- FROM THE EDITORS OF THE BEST RECIPES TEST KITCHEN -

QUICK AND EASY MEALS
SIMPLE RECIPES FOR EVERYDAY LIFE

Best Recipes.co

QUICK AND EASY MEALS
SIMPLE RECIPES FOR EVERYDAY LIFE

**FROM THE EDITORS OF THE
BEST RECIPES TEST KITCHEN**

Copyright © 2020 by
Best Recipes Media Group, LLC

All rights reserved. No part of this book may be reproduced or used, in any form or by any means, electronic or mechanical, without the permission in writing from the publisher.

Published in the United States by
Best Recipes Media Group, LLC

Best Recipes Media Group, LLC publishes its books in a variety of electronic and print formats. Some content that appears in print may not be available in electronic books, and vice versa.

www.bestrecipes.co

Some photographs and recipes in this book originally appeared in previous publications of Best Recipes Magazine.

ISBN: Print 978-0-9987812-3-5

eBook 978-0-9987812-4-2

Printed in China

Cover and Book Design by Drew Maresco

Cover Photography by Drew Maresco and Cheryl Maresco

10 9 8 7 6 5 4 3 2 1

First Edition

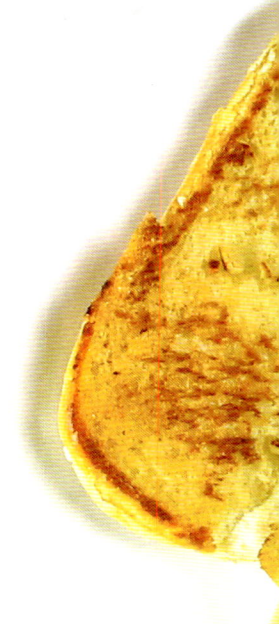

> THIS BOOK IS DEDICATED TO EVERYONE WHO IS LOOKING FOR DELICIOUS RECIPES THEY CAN FEEL GOOD ABOUT FEEDING TO THEIR FAMILIES.

CONTENTS

Introduction 8

Asian 10

Burgers & Sandwiches 32

Pasta 54

Salads 78

Seafood 100

Tex Mex 118

Vegetarian 136

Soups 154

Acknowledgments 177

About the Authors 179

Index 180

INTRODUCTION

As discussions for this book began, we knew we wanted the focus to be on meals that are quick to cook and easy to put together. We thought about you, our reader, and the frustrations that can come from just trying to get dinner on the table in a reasonable amount of time.

Some publications use shortcut ingredients that make you unsure of what you're feeding your family. Or the recipes are so complicated that you have to dedicate 8 hours to it — and it's not even a slow cooker recipe! It just feels like no one gets what they need. Well, we say no more!

With Quick and Easy Meals, we're going back to the basics. We've stripped away any complicated steps and hard-to-find ingredients. With simple, step-by-step instructions and fresh, easy-to-find ingredients, you'll be able to prepare a delicious meal the whole family will love. Most of these recipes come together in under 45 minutes — without sacrificing flavor or quality. We encourage you to make each recipe your own and make any substitutions you'd like along the way!

Recipes with fewer steps mean you're that much closer to getting dinner on the table and spending time with the ones you love. It's as simple as that. Whether you're a kitchen pro or a complete beginner, you'll find these Quick and Easy Meals to be approachable and anxiety-free — just the way cooking should be.

We love to see what you're cooking! Share your recipe creations with us on Instagram @ bestrecipes.co and using our hashtag #quickandeasybr

DREW MARESCO
Editor in chief

THE RECIPE FOR SUCCESS

Whether you're a seasoned pro or just a beginner, our goal is to be more than just another cookbook on your shelf. Join our free online resource made just for you. A place where you can connect with the editors, get free bonus content, and access our online food community. Visit **qae.bestrecipes.co** to sign up or to get more information.

SCAN ME

MEATBALL MARINARA SUBMARINE SANDWICHES PAGE 47

RECIPES

Asian Seared Salmon with Baby Bok Choy	13
Banh Mi with Sriracha Mayo	15
Beef and Broccoli	17
Teriyaki Chicken	19
Sticky Pork Sliders	21
Spicy Chicken Lo Mein	23
Sweet and Sour Chicken	25
Pineapple Fried Rice	27
Quick Pepper Steak	29
Thai Green Curry	31

This chapter is dedicated to helping you explore some amazing Asian-inspired dishes made right in your own kitchen! If this is your first time experimenting with Asian cuisine at home, then you're in for a real treat. You're cooking with pretty high heat, so dinner comes together fast! No wok? No problem! We made all these recipes in our everyday skillets (both cast iron and non-stick), and they turned out beautifully. From classic Chinese takeout favorites, like Sweet and Sour Chicken, Beef and Broccoli, and Thai Green Curry. You'll be inspired to skip the takeout menu and try some adventuresome, from-scratch cooking at home!

ASIAN

SPICY CHICKEN LO MEIN PAGE 23

ASIAN

ASIAN SEARED SALMON WITH BABY BOK CHOY

SERVES 4

Salmon is not only one of the most protein-dense fish in the sea, but it's also a great source of heart-healthy omega-3 fatty acids. We pair it with baby bok choy, and sear them both in the same pan, making sure none of the delicious honey soy sauce goes to waste. The reward? A dinner rich in flavor, and salmon that remains moist and tender.

INGREDIENTS

- 2 cups water
- 1 cup uncooked basmati rice
- ¼ cup low-sodium soy sauce
- ¼ cup honey
- 2 teaspoons toasted sesame oil
- 1 teaspoon canola oil
- 4 (6-ounce) salmon fillets
- ½ teaspoon pepper
- 2 pounds baby bok choy, halved lengthwise
- 1 tablespoon toasted sesame seeds

DIRECTIONS

1 In a medium pot, bring the water to a boil. Add the rice, return to a boil, then cover and reduce the heat to low, cooking for 15-20 minutes, or until the rice is tender. Meanwhile, in a small bowl, stir together the soy sauce, honey, and sesame oil. Arrange the salmon fillets in a shallow dish, season with pepper, then cover with half the sauce.

2 In a large skillet over medium heat, warm the oil. Add the salmon and sear skin-side up for 4 minutes. Pour the remaining sauce into the skillet, swirling around to help release the salmon from the pan if it's sticking. Carefully turn the salmon over, spoon some of the sauce from the pan over the salmon, and continue cooking for another 4 minutes, or until cooked through. Leaving the sauce in the skillet, transfer the salmon to a plate, tent with foil to keep warm, and set aside.

3 Add the bok choy to the skillet, cut side down, and cook 2 minutes per side. Remove the bok choy and reduce the sauce, cooking about 2 minutes. Serve salmon fillets over rice with bok choy on the side. Drizzle with reduced sauce. Garnish with the sesame seeds.

Note: Want more sauce? Simply double the amount of soy sauce, honey, and sesame oil!

ASIAN

BANH MI WITH SRIRACHA MAYO

SERVES 4

Banh Mi is a French-inspired Vietnamese sandwich served on a baguette that's quickly growing in popularity in the US. While they come in many versions, most will have pork, vegetables, and mayo. Our version features juicy marinated pork tenderloin, homemade Sriracha mayo, and a fresh, quick-pickled slaw to round it all out. It makes a great on-the-go lunch or casual dinner that's sure to leave everyone satisfied — and impressed!

BANH MI

- 2 tablespoons low-sodium soy sauce
- 2 tablespoons brown sugar
- 1 teaspoon toasted sesame oil
- 1 teaspoon canola oil
- 2 garlic cloves, minced
- ½ teaspoon ground ginger
- 1½ pounds pork tenderloin, cut into long thin strips
- 2 (12-inch) French baguettes, halved lengthwise

SLAW

- 1 large English cucumber, peeled into ribbons with a vegetable peeler
- 1 carrot, peeled into ribbons
- 1 jalapeño chile, seeded and sliced lengthwise
- 1 green onion, white and light green parts only, thinly sliced
- 3 tablespoons sugar
- 3 tablespoons rice vinegar

SRIRACHA MAYO

- ½ cup mayo
- 3 tablespoons Sriracha
- 1 tablespoon hoisin sauce
- ½ teaspoon garlic powder

DIRECTIONS

1 Preheat the oven to 400°F. In a large bowl, stir together the soy sauce, brown sugar, sesame oil, canola oil, garlic, and ginger. Add the pork to the marinade and let sit for 5 minutes.

2 Meanwhile, in a medium bowl, toss together the cucumber, carrot, jalapeño, green onion, sugar, and vinegar; cover and set aside. In a separate small bowl, stir together the mayo, Sriracha, hoisin sauce, and garlic powder. Set aside.

3 In a large pan over medium-high heat, working in batches to avoid overcrowding, add the pork strips. Cook for about 3-5 minutes per side, or until browned and cooked through. Transfer the finished strips to a plate and continue working in batches until all the pork is cooked.

4 Meanwhile, cut the baguettes in half horizontally, and place them in the oven for 3-5 minutes or until lightly toasted.

5 To serve, spread the mayo on the baguettes, add the pork strips, and top with slaw.

ASIAN

BEEF AND BROCCOLI

SERVES 4

When you think about the typical Chinese takeout, the chances are good that beef and broccoli is one of the first things that comes to mind. With deep savory flavors and simple ingredients, it's hard to go wrong with such a delicious yet traditional meal.

SAUCE

- ¼ cup low-sodium soy sauce
- 3 tablespoons oyster sauce
- 1 tablespoon brown sugar
- 1 teaspoon toasted sesame oil
- 1 tablespoon rice wine vinegar
- 1 teaspoon powdered ginger
- 4 garlic cloves, sliced

BEEF AND BROCCOLI

- 4 cups water
- 2 cups uncooked basmati rice
- 1 tablespoon canola oil
- 2 medium onions, finely diced
- 1 pound sirloin, cut into 1-inch cubes
- 1 head broccoli, cut into small florets

DIRECTIONS

1 In a medium bowl, stir together the soy sauce, oyster sauce, brown sugar, sesame oil, rice wine vinegar, ginger, and garlic. Set aside.

2 In a medium pot, bring the water to a boil. Add the rice, return to a boil, then cover and reduce the heat to low, cooking for 15-20 minutes, or until the rice is tender.

3 Meanwhile, in a large pan over medium-high heat, warm the oil. Add the onions and cook, stirring continuously until translucent, about 4-5 minutes. Transfer the onions to a bowl, cover, and set aside.

4 Add the sirloin to the pan and cook for about 4-5 minutes on each side, or until lightly browned. Return the onions back to the pan, add the broccoli, and continue cooking for about 3-4 minutes, stirring occasionally. Lower the heat to medium, add the sauce, and cook for another 3-5 minutes, or until the sauce has thickened. Serve over the rice.

ASIAN

TERIYAKI CHICKEN

SERVES 4

This famous Japanese dish is stir-fried to perfection and glazed in a beautifully flavored, homemade teriyaki sauce. You'll ask yourself why you ever spent the money on a delivery fee when it's so easy to make at home.

SAUCE

- ¼ cup low-sodium soy sauce
- 2 tablespoons honey
- 2 tablespoons dry sherry
- 2 tablespoons rice wine vinegar
- 1 tablespoon cornstarch
- 2 garlic cloves, minced
- ½ teaspoon sesame oil
- ¼ teaspoon ground ginger

CHICKEN

- 4 cups water
- 2 cups uncooked basmati rice
- 1 pound boneless, skinless chicken breasts, cut into 1-inch cubes
- ½ teaspoon salt
- ¼ teaspoon pepper
- 1 tablespoon canola oil
- 1 cup snow peas
- 1 cup baby bok choy, chopped
- Sesame seeds, to garnish
- Green onions, sliced, to garnish

DIRECTIONS

1 In a large bowl, whisk together the soy sauce, honey, dry sherry, rice wine vinegar, cornstarch, garlic, sesame oil, and ginger. Set aside.

2 In a medium pot, bring the water to a boil. Add the rice, return to a boil, then cover and reduce the heat to low, cooking for 15-20 minutes, or until the rice is tender.

3 Season the chicken with salt and pepper. In a large pan over medium-high heat, warm the oil. Add the chicken to the pan, cooking 3-4 minutes per side, or until opaque. Add the snow peas and bok choy, stirring continuously for 2-3 minutes. Reduce the heat to medium, add the sauce to the pan, and cook until the sauce has thickened, about 4-5 minutes.

4 Serve the chicken over rice. Top with sesame seeds and green onions as desired.

ASIAN

STICKY PORK SLIDERS

YIELD 12 | SERVES 4

They aren't called sticky for nothing! The pork is cooked in a savory sauce enriched with honey and brown sugar that's sweet, salty, a little spicy, and definitely sticky! Served on a traditional Chinese bao bun and topped with a fresh slaw, these little sliders will have you going back for seconds.

SLAW

- 1 cup coleslaw mix
- 2 pickling cucumbers, sliced into thin matchsticks
- 2 green onions, thinly sliced
- 1 celery stalk, sliced into thin matchsticks
- ¼ cup chopped cilantro
- 1 tablespoon rice wine vinegar
- 1 tablespoon sugar

PORK

- 1 cup chicken broth
- ¼ cup low-sodium soy sauce
- 3 tablespoons honey
- 2 tablespoons brown sugar
- 2 tablespoons dry sherry
- 3 garlic cloves, minced
- 1 jalapeño chile, thinly sliced or minced
- 1 tablespoon powdered ginger
- 1 tablespoon canola oil
- 2 pounds pork shoulder roast, cut into 1-inch pieces
- 12 steamed bao buns or slider buns

DIRECTIONS

1 In a medium bowl, gently stir together the coleslaw mix, cucumber, green onions, celery, cilantro, vinegar, and sugar. Cover and set aside until ready to serve.

2 In a medium bowl, stir together the chicken broth, soy sauce, honey, brown sugar, sherry, garlic, jalapeño, and ginger. Set aside.

3 In a large pan over medium heat, warm the oil. Add the pork, cooking about 4-5 minutes per side, or until lightly browned and cooked through.

4 Reduce the heat to medium-low, add the sauce to the pork, cover and let simmer for 15 minutes, stirring occasionally. Move the pork and sauce to a large bowl. Using two forks, shred the pork and stir to coat with the sauce.

5 To serve, fill steamed bao buns with sticky pork mixture and top with slaw.

ASIAN

SPICY CHICKEN LO MEIN

SERVES 6

This quick and easy lo mein is a simple dish with big flavor. Featuring an assortment of colorful vegetables, it's a great way to satisfy a Chinese food craving right in your own kitchen.

SAUCE

- ⅔ cup low-sodium soy sauce
- 3 garlic cloves, minced
- 3 tablespoons sugar
- 2 tablespoons oyster sauce
- 2 teaspoons toasted sesame oil
- 2 teaspoons powdered ginger
- 2 teaspoons Sriracha, plus more to taste

LO MEIN

- 1 pound Chinese egg noodles or spaghetti
- 1 tablespoon canola oil
- 1 medium onion, cut into ¼-inch thick slices
- 2 pounds boneless skinless chicken thighs, cut into ½-inch cubes
- 1 red bell pepper, thinly sliced
- 2 carrots, thinly sliced
- 2 celery stalks, diagonally sliced
- 1 (5-ounce) can sliced water chestnuts

DIRECTIONS

1 In a small bowl, stir together soy sauce, garlic, sugar, oyster sauce, sesame oil, ginger, and Sriracha. Set aside.

2 Bring a large pot of water to a boil, add the pasta. and cook according to the package directions. Drain and set aside.

3 Meanwhile, in a large pan over medium-high heat, warm the oil. Add the onions and cook for about 7 minutes, stirring frequently, until soft and translucent. Transfer the onions to a bowl and set aside.

4 Add half of the chicken to the pan, cooking for about 3-4 minutes per side, or until cooked through. Transfer to a plate and cook the remaining chicken. Remove from the pan when done.

5 Add the peppers, carrots, celery, and water chestnuts to the pan and cook for 3-5 minutes, stirring occasionally. Return the onions and chicken to the pan, then add the sauce and prepared noodles. Stir together until the sauce is fully absorbed, about 3-5 minutes.

ASIAN

SWEET AND SOUR CHICKEN

SERVES 6

As a typical fan favorite, and it doesn't take long to turn out this classic. With its signature sweet and tangy flavors, what more could you want from a traditional Chinese dinner at home?

SAUCE

- ½ cup chicken broth
- ½ cup pineapple juice (reserved from canned pineapple)
- ½ cup light brown sugar
- ¼ cup Chinese rice wine vinegar
- ¼ cup ketchup
- 1 teaspoon grated fresh ginger, or ½ teaspoon dried ginger
- 2 tablespoons cornstarch, mixed with 2 tablespoons water

CHICKEN

- 4 cups water
- 2 cups uncooked basmati rice
- 1 teaspoon salt
- ½ teaspoon pepper
- 2 pounds boneless, skinless chicken thighs, cut into 1-inch cubes
- 1 tablespoon canola oil
- 1 red pepper, chopped
- ½ pound snow peas, ends trimmed
- 3 green onions, cut into 1-inch pieces
- 1 cup canned pineapple chunks, drained

DIRECTIONS

1 In a medium bowl, whisk together the chicken broth, pineapple juice, brown sugar, rice wine vinegar, ketchup, ginger, and cornstarch mixture. Set aside.

2 In a medium pot, bring the water to a boil. Add the rice, return to a boil, then cover and reduce the heat to low, cooking for 15-20 minutes, or until the rice is tender.

3 Season the chicken with salt and pepper. In a large pan over medium heat, warm the oil. Add the chicken, cooking about 5-6 minutes per side, or until the chicken is cooked through. Add the peppers, snow peas, onions, pineapple, and sauce. Cook 3-4 minutes, stirring occasionally, until the sauce has thickened. Serve over the rice.

Quick and Easy Meals

ASIAN

PINEAPPLE FRIED RICE

SERVES 4

Fried rice is one of the most popular dishes ordered at Chinese takeout restaurants. In our version, we added a sweet twist by adding pineapple for you to enjoy. The pineapple brings a sweet and juicy contrast to the savory sauce in this delightful, vegetable-loaded dinner.

SAUCE

- ¼ cup low-sodium soy sauce
- 2 tablespoons toasted sesame oil
- 1 tablespoon brown sugar
- 2 garlic cloves, minced
- 1 teaspoon powdered ginger
- ¼ teaspoon pepper

INGREDIENTS

- 2 tablespoons canola oil
- 1 medium onion, diced
- 2 carrots, peeled and grated
- ½ cup frozen corn
- ½ cup frozen peas
- 3 cups cooked basmati rice (preferably refrigerated overnight)
- 2 cups diced fresh pineapple
- 2 green onions, sliced diagonally

DIRECTIONS

1 In a small bowl, whisk together soy sauce, sesame oil, brown sugar, garlic, ginger, and pepper. Set aside.

2 In a large pan over medium heat, warm the oil. Add the onions and cook about 3-4 minutes, stirring often, until they become translucent. Add the carrots, corn, and peas to the pan, cooking about 3-4 minutes, until the vegetables are tender. Stir in the cooked rice, pineapple, green onions, and soy sauce mixture, stirring constantly. Cook about 4 minutes, until heated through.

Note: Fresh cooked rice works here as well, but pre-cooking and refrigerating the rice a day ahead gives you the texture most desired in a fried rice dish. To ensure food safety, be sure to spread the rice in a shallow layer before refrigerating, so it cools quickly.

ASIAN

QUICK PEPPER STEAK

SERVES 4

This Chinese-American dinner is a wonderful stir-fried dish with steak, bell peppers, onions, and a well-rounded, flavorful sauce. Even picky eaters are going to enjoy this soon-to-be kitchen staple!

SAUCE

- 3 cups beef broth
- 4 tablespoons cornstarch
- 3 tablespoons low-sodium soy sauce
- 2 garlic cloves, minced
- ½ teaspoon powdered ginger
- 1 tablespoon sugar

INGREDIENTS

- 6 cups water
- 3 cups uncooked basmati rice
- 1 tablespoon canola oil
- 1 medium onion, cut into wedges
- 1 pound sirloin steak, sliced thin across the grain
- 2 large green peppers, sliced

DIRECTIONS

1 In a small bowl, stir together the broth, cornstarch, soy sauce, garlic, ginger, and sugar until smooth. Set aside.

2 In a medium pot, bring the water to a boil. Add the rice, return to a boil, then cover and reduce the heat to low, cooking for 15-20 minutes, or until the rice is tender.

3 In a medium pan over medium-high heat, warm the oil. Add the onion, cooking about 5-7 minutes, until translucent. Add the beef to the pan and cook about 8 minutes, or until cooked through and lightly browned, stirring occasionally.

4 Reduce the heat to medium, add the peppers, and cook for 5 minutes. Add the sauce and cook for 5 minutes, or until the sauce has thickened. Serve over the rice.

ASIAN

THAI GREEN CURRY

SERVES 4

This rich green curry gets its hue from cilantro and its fresh flavor from the ginger and lemongrass. With a touch of heat and a cooling contrast from the coconut cream, this curry makes for a delicious and satisfying meal.

CURRY PASTE

- 1 cup chopped fresh cilantro
- 3 tablespoons canola oil
- 1 stalk lemongrass, minced (or 2 tablespoons bottled lemongrass)
- 1 tablespoon low-sodium soy sauce
- 2 jalapeño chilies, seeded (omit if heat is not desired)
- 4 green onions, quartered
- 4 garlic cloves
- 1 (1-inch) piece fresh ginger, peeled
- 1 teaspoon brown sugar
- ½ teaspoon cumin
- ½ teaspoon salt
- ¼ teaspoon pepper

INGREDIENTS

- 2 cups water
- 1 cup uncooked basmati rice
- 1 tablespoon canola oil
- 4 boneless skinless chicken thighs, cut into 1-inch cubes
- 1 (14-ounce) can coconut milk
- ½ pound snow peas, ends trimmed
- ½ cup chicken broth or water
- 1 large lime, cut into wedges

DIRECTIONS

1 In a food processor, fitted with an "S" blade, add the cilantro, oil, lemongrass, soy sauce, jalapeños, green onion, garlic, ginger, brown sugar, cumin, salt, and pepper. Process until smooth, about 1 minute. Set aside.

2 In a medium pot, bring the water to a boil. Add the rice, return to a boil, then cover and reduce the heat to low, cooking for 15-20 minutes, or until the rice is tender.

3 Meanwhile, in a large pan over medium-high heat, warm the oil. Add the chicken, stirring until almost cooked through, about 5-6 minutes. Stir in the prepared curry paste, coconut milk, and chicken broth (or water). Bring to a simmer and cook for 3 minutes. Add the snow peas, reduce the heat to medium-low, and simmer for another 3 minutes. Serve over rice and garnish with lime wedges.

RECIPES

Aloha BBQ Burger Sliders	35
Black Bean Quinoa Burger	37
Cajun Shrimp Po' Boy	39
Chicken Parm Sandwich	41
Fiesta Chicken Burger	43
Lemon Chicken Pita Wraps with Tzatziki	45
Meatball Marinara Submarine Sandwiches	47
Mediterranean Meatballs	49
Philly Cheesesteak	51
Pimento Cheeseburgers	53

You may not think of burgers and sandwiches as a dinnertime main course, but we beg to differ. In this chapter, you'll get a wide variety of flavor profiles, from Fiesta Chicken Burgers and Shrimp Po' Boys to vegetarian options like Black Bean Quinoa Burgers that even the biggest meat-eater will love. And speaking of meat, we've got Philly Cheesesteaks and Meatball Subs, too. You will be taken by surprise by the sheer ease that comes with making burgers and sandwiches into dinner perfection!

BURGERS & SANDWICHES

PIMENTO CHEESEBURGERS PAGE 53

BURGERS & SANDWICHES

ALOHA BBQ BURGER SLIDERS

YIELD 12 | SERVES 4

We gave the simple slider a Hawaiian twist by loading these burgers with pineapple, BBQ sauce, and grilled red onion. Bursting with fresh flavor, this is a dish that you'll want to make time and time again!

INGREDIENTS

- 1½ pounds ground beef
- ⅔ cup BBQ sauce, divided
- 1 teaspoon salt
- ¼ teaspoon pepper
- ¼ teaspoon garlic powder
- ¼ teaspoon paprika
- ¼ teaspoon onion powder
- ⅛ teaspoon dried thyme
- 1 small red onion, thinly sliced
- 1 (12-ounce) package sweet dinner rolls
- 1½ tablespoons canola oil, divided
- 3 slices swiss cheese, quartered
- 1 (8-ounce) can pineapple slices, drained, cut into thirds

DIRECTIONS

1 In a large bowl, using clean hands, combine the beef, ⅓ cup barbecue sauce, salt, pepper, garlic powder, paprika, onion powder, and thyme. Shape the mixture into 12 evenly-sized small patties. Cover and refrigerate if not grilling immediately.

2 Preheat the grill or a grill pan to medium heat and warm ½ tablespoon of the oil. Add the onions and grill until they begin to turn translucent, about 4-5 minutes. Move the onions to the side and add the burgers to the grill, cooking 3-4 minutes per side, or until browned. Transfer to a clean plate.

3 Remove the rolls from the package and, without separating them, cut the entire loaf in half horizontally. Brush the cut sides with the remaining oil and toast, oiled side down on the grill, about 2 minutes. Transfer the rolls to a platter, spread with the remaining ⅓ cup of barbecue sauce, then separate the rolls. Place the patties on the bottom halves of the rolls, top with cheese, pineapple, and red onions. Add the tops of rolls and serve.

Quick and Easy Meals

BURGERS & SANDWICHES

BLACK BEAN QUINOA BURGER

SERVES 4

If you think bean burgers sound boring, then we implore you to give these a try! Perfect for a Meatless Monday or to impress a vegetarian friend, this isn't your average bean burger. Loaded with flavor and an almost meat-like texture, you won't be asking, "Where's the beef?"

INGREDIENTS

- 1 medium carrot, peeled and chopped
- 1 small red onion, diced
- 2 garlic cloves
- 2 tablespoons chopped fresh cilantro
- 1 teaspoon salt
- ½ teaspoon pepper
- 1 (15-ounce) can black beans, drained
- ½ cup cooked quinoa
- 1 egg or 1 flax "egg" (1 tablespoon flax seed mixed with 3 tablespoons warm water)
- ¼ cup nutritional yeast
- 1 tablespoon Worcestershire sauce
- 1 teaspoon lime juice
- ¼ teaspoon cumin
- ¼ teaspoon chili powder
- ½ cup panko breadcrumbs
- 1 teaspoon canola oil
- 4 hamburger buns

OPTIONAL TOPPINGS

Tomato slices
Shredded lettuce
Cheese slices
Mayo
Mustard
Ketchup

DIRECTIONS

1 In a food processor fitted with an "S" blade, pulse the carrots, red onion, garlic, cilantro, salt, and pepper together until finely minced. In a large bowl, combine the processed veggies, beans, and quinoa.

2 In a medium bowl, whisk together the egg (or flax egg substitute), nutritional yeast, Worcestershire sauce, lime juice, cumin, chili powder, and breadcrumbs; add to the bean mixture in the large bowl and stir to combine. Using clean hands, form the mixture into 4 patties.

3 Preheat a grill pan over medium heat, brush with oil, and lay the patties on the grill, cooking about 6-8 minutes per side. Serve on buns with your choice of toppings.

BURGERS & SANDWICHES

CAJUN SHRIMP PO' BOY

SERVES 4

A traditional sandwich from Louisiana, this version is packed with flavor and a touch of heat — but not too much! You start by making a Cajun seasoning that's so good you're going to be glad that there's plenty left over to use in other recipes. A homemade tartar sauce contrasts the heat, cooling things off with a bit of tang. It's a mouth-watering sandwich you're sure to love!

TARTAR SAUCE

- 1 cup mayo
- 1 tablespoon lemon juice
- 1 tablespoon Worcestershire sauce
- 1 tablespoon sweet pickle relish
- 1 teaspoon onion powder

CAJUN SEASONING

- 2 teaspoons salt
- 2 teaspoons garlic powder
- 1 teaspoon pepper
- 1 teaspoon onion powder
- ½ teaspoon cayenne pepper
- 1 teaspoon dried oregano
- 1 teaspoon dried thyme
- 1 teaspoons paprika

PO' BOY INGREDIENTS

- 2 tablespoons Cajun seasoning
- 1 pound shrimp, peeled and deveined
- 2 teaspoons canola oil
- ½ cup shredded romaine lettuce
- 1 tomato, thinly sliced
- 1 red onion, thinly sliced
- 4 hoagie rolls

DIRECTIONS

1 In a small bowl, stir together the mayo, lemon juice, Worcestershire sauce, relish, and onion powder; cover and chill until ready for use.

2 In a medium bowl, whisk together the salt, garlic powder, pepper, onion powder, cayenne, oregano, thyme, and paprika. Reserve 2 tablespoons of the seasoning mix and store the rest in an airtight container for future use.

3 In a large bowl, toss the shrimp with the reserved Cajun seasoning. In a large pan over medium-high heat, warm the oil and add the shrimp, cooking about 2 minutes per side or until opaque.

4 Set oven to broil on high. Open the hoagie rolls, lay them cut side up on a baking sheet, and broil for 3 minutes, or until toasted. Spread the tartar sauce on the rolls, layer with lettuce, tomato, onion, and a generous amount of shrimp.

Quick and Easy Meals

BURGERS & SANDWICHES

CHICKEN PARM SANDWICH

SERVES 6

Chicken Parmesan is an Italian favorite, and we gave it a fun twist by turning it into a sandwich. We lightened this up by toasting the panko, guaranteeing you the crunch you are looking for, without the frying. The melty mozzarella cheese makes this sandwich an Italian food lover's on-the-go dream!

INGREDIENTS

- 2 cups panko breadcrumbs
- ½ cup grated parmesan cheese
- 2 eggs
- ⅓ cup flour
- 3 boneless, skinless chicken breasts, cut in half lengthwise and pounded to ½-inch thick cutlets
- 1 teaspoon salt
- ½ teaspoon pepper
- 2 cups marinara sauce
- 16 ounces shredded or fresh mozzarella cheese
- 6 ciabatta buns

DIRECTIONS

1 Preheat the oven to 400°F. Spread the breadcrumbs in a thin layer on a baking sheet. Toast for about 4 minutes, or until lightly browned.

2 In a shallow bowl, toss together the toasted panko and parmesan cheese. In a second shallow bowl, beat the eggs. Add the flour to a resealable bag. Season the chicken with salt and pepper.

3 Place two chicken cutlets in the bag with the flour, close the bag, and shake to thoroughly coat. Remove each chicken cutlet from the bag, shaking off any excess flour. Dip into the egg on both sides, then transfer to the panko mixture, pressing to make sure the crumbs stick. Gently shake off any excess crumbs and place the cutlets on a baking sheet lined with a wire rack. Repeat with the remaining cutlets — cook for 12 minutes.

4 Remove from the oven and spoon an even amount of marinara sauce on to each cutlet. Top the cutlets with mozzarella cheese, and return to the oven. Cook for 5-7 minutes, or until the chicken is cooked through and the cheese is melted. Serve on ciabatta buns.

BURGERS & SANDWICHES

FIESTA CHICKEN BURGER

SERVES 4

Sometimes life needs a little spice! When you're not in the mood for just a regular burger, this recipe is here to awaken your taste buds with a kick and a crunch. Chicken (or turkey) makes it a little leaner than a beef burger, so you can feel great while piling it high with flavorful pepper jack cheese, avocado, and corn chips. It's a fiesta in every bite!

INGREDIENTS

- ½ cup mayo
- 1 tablespoon lime juice
- 1 pound ground chicken or turkey
- ½ cup plain, dried breadcrumbs
- 1½ teaspoons seasoned salt
- ½ teaspoon chili powder
- ¼ teaspoon cayenne pepper
- 2 garlic cloves, minced
- 1 teaspoon canola oil
- 4 brioche buns
- 4 slices pepper jack cheese
- 1 avocado, sliced
- Corn chips

DIRECTIONS

1 In a small bowl, stir together the mayo and lime juice. Place in the refrigerator until ready to serve.

2 In a medium bowl, using clean hands, combine the ground chicken or turkey, breadcrumbs, seasoned salt, chili powder, cayenne pepper, and garlic. Divide and shape the mixture into 4 equal patties. Refrigerate until ready to cook.

3 Preheat the grill or a grill pan over medium-high heat. Lightly oil the grill, or warm the oil in the grill pan, add the patties, and cook for about 6 minutes per side, or until the internal temperature reaches 165°F. Serve the burgers on buns topped with pepper jack cheese, lime mayo, avocado slices, and corn chips.

BURGERS & SANDWICHES

LEMON CHICKEN PITA WRAPS WITH TZATZIKI

SERVES 4

Flavorful and protein-packed, these Greek-inspired sandwiches are sure to be a favorite. Cooling tzatziki adds vibrant freshness to the warm seasoned chicken and sliced tomatoes in a wrap full of satisfying flavors.

TZATZIKI

- 1 (10-ounce) package plain Greek yogurt
- 1 medium cucumber, peeled, seeded, and finely diced
- 2 teaspoons lemon juice
- 1 teaspoon chopped fresh dill
- 1 garlic clove, minced
- ½ teaspoon salt
- ¼ teaspoon pepper

INGREDIENTS

- 3 boneless, skinless chicken breasts, cut into 1-inch cubes
- 2 teaspoons dried oregano
- 2 teaspoons lemon zest
- ½ teaspoon salt
- ¼ teaspoon pepper
- 4 teaspoons canola oil
- 3 large ripe tomatoes, sliced
- 4 pita flatbreads

DIRECTIONS

1 In a medium bowl, stir together the Greek yogurt, cucumber, lemon juice, dill, garlic, salt, and pepper until thoroughly combined. Set aside.

2 In a large bowl, toss together the cubed chicken, oregano, lemon zest, salt, and pepper.

3 In a large pan over medium-high heat, warm the oil. Add the chicken in a single layer, cooking for about 3-4 minutes per side, until the chicken is fully cooked. Serve the chicken in warm pitas with sliced tomatoes and tzatziki sauce.

BURGERS & SANDWICHES

MEATBALL MARINARA SUBMARINE SANDWICHES

SERVES 4

Mouth-watering, easy to make, and tender. While a meatball sub may not sound revolutionary, that doesn't mean it can't be delicious! A simple marinara sauce cooks these delicate meatballs to perfection. Be sure to keep extra napkins nearby!

INGREDIENTS

- 1 pound ground beef
- 1 cup fresh breadcrumbs
- ⅓ cup water
- 1 large egg, lightly beaten
- 1 tablespoon + ½ teaspoon dried oregano
- 1 teaspoon salt
- ¼ teaspoon pepper
- 3 tablespoons olive oil
- 2 garlic cloves, minced
- 1 (28-ounce) can tomato puree
- 1 (15-ounce) can diced tomatoes
- 3 tablespoons fresh chopped basil (4-6 leaves)
- 4 French or Italian rolls
- 1 cup shredded mozzarella cheese
-   Grated parmesan cheese

DIRECTIONS

1 In a large bowl, using clean hands, combine the beef, breadcrumbs, water, egg, 1 tablespoon of oregano, salt, and pepper. Gently form the mixture into 12 meatballs.

2 In a large pot over medium heat, add the oil and minced garlic, cook for about 1-2 minutes, until fragrant, but not browned. Stir in the tomato puree, diced tomatoes, basil, and remaining ½ teaspoon of oregano. Bring to a boil, then reduce to a light simmer. Add the meatballs, cover, and simmer for 10-15 minutes, until cooked through.

3 Serve with 3 meatballs and some marinara on each roll, topped with mozzarella and parmesan cheeses.

Quick and Easy Meals

BURGERS & SANDWICHES

MEDITERRANEAN MEATBALLS

SERVES 4

These meatballs are flavor-packed with Mediterranean seasonings! Their richness pairs perfectly with the tangy homemade tzatziki sauce. If you're looking for a little flair without the fuss, these sandwiches — served on warm, soft pitas — are it!

TZATZIKI SAUCE

- 10 ounces plain Greek yogurt
- ½ large cucumber, peeled, seeded, and finely diced
- 2 teaspoons lemon juice
- Salt and pepper, to taste
- 1 teaspoon chopped fresh dill
- 1 clove garlic, minced

INGREDIENTS

- 1 pound ground beef
- ¼ cup dry breadcrumbs
- 1 egg
- 3 garlic cloves, minced
- 2 teaspoons dried basil
- 2 teaspoons dried oregano
- 1 teaspoon ground cinnamon
- 1 teaspoon dried parsley
- 1 teaspoon dried rosemary, minced
- 1 teaspoon salt
- ½ teaspoon pepper
- ½ teaspoon cumin
- 4 Greek-style flatbread pitas
- ½ large cucmber, diced
- 1 large tomato, chopped
- 2 teaspoons fresh dill
- 2 teaspoons fresh parsley

DIRECTIONS

1 Preheat the oven to 425°F. In a medium bowl, stir together the yogurt, half of the cucumber, lemon juice, salt, pepper, dill, and garlic. Set aside.

2 In a large mixing bowl, using clean hands, combine the beef, breadcrumbs, egg, garlic, basil, oregano, cinnamon, parsley, rosemary, salt, pepper, and cumin. Form into 1-inch balls and place on a rimmed baking sheet. Cook for 15 minutes, turning halfway through, or until browned.

3 Remove the meatballs from the oven and rest for 3 minutes before serving. Add some tzatziki sauce to a pita, top with 3-4 meatballs, garnish with remaining cucumber, tomato, dill, and parsley, then roll closed.

Quick and Easy Meals

BURGERS & SANDWICHES

PHILLY CHEESESTEAK

SERVES 6

Just like its name states, the Philly cheesesteak originated in Philadelphia. Loaded up with peppers and caramelized onions, it's no wonder these sandwiches became a hit nationwide. Now you can try making these famous sandwiches right at home!

INGREDIENTS

- 1 teaspoon canola oil
- 1 medium onion, sliced
- 1 red pepper, sliced
- 1 green pepper, sliced
- 1½ pounds sirloin or ribeye beef, cut into ¼-inch, or thinner, strips
- 1 teaspoon garlic powder
- ½ teaspoon salt
- ½ teaspoon pepper
- ½ teaspoon Worcestershire sauce
- 1 tablespoon low-sodium soy sauce
- 6 hoagie rolls, sliced lengthwise and toasted
- 6 slices provolone cheese

DIRECTIONS

1 In a large pan over medium-high heat, warm the oil. Add the onions and peppers, cooking about 12-15 minutes, or until soft. Remove from the pan and set aside.

2 Season the beef with garlic powder, salt, and pepper. Add the beef to the pan and cook for about 4-5 minutes per side. Add the Worcestershire sauce and soy sauce, return the onions and peppers to the pan and toss to coat. Continue cooking for 2 minutes or until heated through. Serve on hoagie rolls, topped with sliced cheese.

Note: Some stores offer shaved beef, which can be used for this recipe as it's what we used in the photo. If using, stir more frequently because the thinner beef will cook much quicker.

BURGERS & SANDWICHES

PIMENTO CHEESEBURGERS

SERVES 6

Juicy burgers piled with melty pimento cheese — it's a simple upgrade from your everyday burger. With a sweet heat kick you just won't be able to resist, these burgers will leave you wanting more.

INGREDIENTS

- 2 cups shredded colby or cheddar cheese
- 1 (4-ounce) jar diced pimentos, drained
- ½ cup mayo
- ¼ teaspoon onion powder
- ¼ teaspoon garlic powder
- ⅛ teaspoon cayenne pepper
- 2 pounds ground chuck
- 1½ teaspoons salt
- 1½ teaspoons pepper
- 1 teaspoon canola oil
- 6 hamburger buns

DIRECTIONS

1 In a small bowl, stir together the cheese, pimentos, mayo, onion powder, garlic powder, and cayenne. Set aside.

2 Using clean hands, add the salt and pepper to the beef and mix well. Divide into 6 patties.

3 Preheat the grill or a grill pan to medium-high heat. Lightly oil the grill, or warm the oil in the grill pan, add the patties, and cook for 4-6 minutes per side, or until browned. Add 3 tablespoons of the pimento cheese mixture to each patty and cover the grill or grill pan, allowing the cheese to melt, about 2 minutes. Serve on the hamburger buns.

Quick and Easy Meals

RECIPES

Carbonara	57
Spaghetti with Chicken Parmesan Meatballs	59
Penne with Lemon Cream Sauce and Spinach	61
Mac and Cheese	63
Orecchiette with Tomato Cream Sauce	65
Meaty Mozzarella Pasta Bake	67
Spaghetti and Meatballs	69
Stroganoff Meatballs	71
Spinach & Ricotta Stuffed Shells	73
Sausage, Sweet Potato, and Kale Pasta	75
Tortellini Alfredo with Bacon	77

Can you think of a better quick fix meal than pasta? It's admittedly one of our favorites for a time-strapped weekday because it's quick to cook and incredibly versatile. We've dedicated this chapter to this incredible timesaver, and included a wide range of flavors to keep things exciting! From cream to tomato sauces including a combination of the two, and toppers like meatballs and veggies, you're going to find a pasta dish just for you. So embrace your inner Italian, and as they say in Italy, "Divertiti, mangiamo!" ("Enjoy yourself, let's eat!")

PASTA

SPAGHETTI WITH CHICKEN PARMESAN MEATBALLS PAGE 59

PASTA

CARBONARA

SERVES 4

What happens when you combine a handful of favorite American breakfast ingredients with spaghetti? In this case, you end up with a classic Italian dish. If you've never had a real carbonara, this recipe may seem a bit unusual to you, but when it's done, we're willing to bet you'll fall for its rich flavor and velvety smooth results.

INGREDIENTS

- 8 slices thick-cut bacon, diced
- 4 eggs
- 1½ cups grated parmesan, plus extra for garnish
- ½ cup heavy cream
- 1 (16-ounce) package spaghetti
- ½ teaspoon pepper
- ¼ teaspoon salt

DIRECTIONS

1 In a medium pan over medium-high heat, cook the bacon until crispy, about 8-12 minutes, stirring occasionally. When done, transfer the bacon to a paper towel-lined plate.

2 In a large bowl, whisk together the eggs, parmesan, and heavy cream. Set aside.

3 Bring a large pot of water to a boil, add the pasta, and cook according to the package directions. Reserve ½ cup of the pasta water for the sauce, then drain and set aside.

4 Immediately transfer the hot pasta to the egg mixture, working quickly to toss. If needed, while mixing, add the pasta water a little at a time to loosen the sauce. Stir in the bacon, salt, and pepper. Serve immediately and top with additional parmesan cheese.

PASTA

SPAGHETTI WITH CHICKEN PARMESAN MEATBALLS

SERVES 4

Everyone knows chicken parmesan! Well, we took the liberty of having a little fun with this one. We shaped ground chicken into meatballs, then stuffed them with melty mozzarella for a twist on classic spaghetti and meatballs that's just downright fun to eat!

INGREDIENTS

- 1 pound ground chicken
- 2 cups dried breadcrumbs, divided
- 3 eggs
- 3 garlic cloves, minced
- 2 teaspoons seasoned salt
- 1 teaspoon chili powder
- 1 teaspoon dried oregano
- 1 teaspoon Italian seasoning
- 8 (1-inch) cubes fresh mozzarella
- 1 cup canola oil
- 1 (16-ounce) package spaghetti noodles
- 1 (20-ounce) jar marinara sauce

DIRECTIONS

1 Preheat the oven to 350°F. In a medium bowl, using clean hands, mix together the ground chicken, 1 cup of breadcrumbs, 1 egg, garlic, seasoned salt, chili powder, oregano, and Italian seasoning. Evenly divide the meat mixture into 8 disks. Place a square of cheese in the middle of each disk, then roll the meat around the cube to make a ball.

2 Place the remaining breadcrumbs into a small bowl. Crack the 2 remaining eggs into a separate small bowl and whisk. Roll each meatball into the egg, then roll in the breadcrumbs.

3 In a medium deep set pan over medium heat, warm the oil until it reaches 350°F on a deep-fry thermometer. Fry the meatballs for about 1 minute per side, until all sides are golden brown. Once the meatballs are golden brown, place them on a baking sheet and bake for 8 minutes.

4 Meanwhile, bring a large pot of water to a boil, add the pasta, and cook according to the package directions. Drain the noodles and return them to the pot until ready to serve. In a small saucepan over medium heat, add the prepared sauce and stir, cooking about 3-4 minutes, until it's warmed through.

5 Divide the spaghetti between four bowls, topping each portion with sauce and two meatballs.

Quick and Easy Meals

PASTA

PENNE WITH LEMON CREAM SAUCE AND SPINACH

SERVES 4

This creamy sauce is very similar to alfredo, just with a lighter feel. The garlic and lemon bring a fresh, bright flavor that shines through its rich creaminess. This sauce will pair well with any summer greens or vine-ripened tomatoes, so don't be afraid to experiment, add ingredients, and make it your own!

INGREDIENTS

- 1 (16-ounce) package penne pasta
- 1 tablespoon canola oil
- 2 garlic cloves, smashed
- 1 lemon, zested and juiced
- 2 cups heavy whipping cream
- ½ teaspoon salt
- ¼ teaspoon pepper
- 1 (4-ounce) bag fresh baby spinach
- ¼ cup parmesan, for garnish

DIRECTIONS

1 Bring a large pot of water to a boil, add the pasta, and cook according to the package directions.

2 Meanwhile, in a medium saucepan over medium-high heat, warm the oil. Add the garlic and cook, stirring, about 1 minute, until fragrant. Reduce the heat to low, add the lemon zest, cream, salt, and pepper; cooking until the sauce is reduced by half, about 10 minutes. Stir in the lemon juice and use a slotted spoon to remove the garlic cloves.

3 Once the pasta is cooked through, drain and immediately return it to the warm pot. Add the spinach and the sauce, stirring until the spinach has wilted. Serve topped with parmesan.

PASTA

MAC AND CHEESE

SERVES 4

There's nothing that says comfort food more than mac and cheese. We've given this dish a grown-makeover, but we promise it will still please your inner child! The gooey melty cheese paired with a crunchy breadcrumb and bacon topping creates a fantastic textural contrast that's sure to please grownups and children alike!

TOPPING

- ½ cup panko breadcrumbs
- ½ cup grated parmesan cheese
- 3 tablespoons butter, melted
- ½ teaspoon paprika
- 8 slices thick-cut bacon, diced

INGREDIENTS

- 1 (16-ounce) package elbow macaroni
- ½ cup butter
- ½ cup flour
- 4 cups milk
- 1 teaspoon salt
- ¼ teaspoon pepper
- 12 ounces shredded cheddar cheese

DIRECTIONS

1 Preheat the oven to 350°F. In a medium bowl, stir together the panko, parmesan, butter, and paprika until well combined. Set aside.

2 In a medium pan set over medium-high heat, cook the bacon until crispy, about 8-12 minutes, stirring occasionally. Transfer the bacon to a paper towel-lined plate.

3 Bring a large pot of water to a boil, add the pasta, and cook according to the package directions. Drain and set aside.

4 Meanwhile, in another large pot, melt the butter over medium heat. Whisk in the flour as the butter begins to bubble. Cook for 3-5 minutes, stirring constantly, until you have a smooth, lightly-browned, peanut butter-colored roux. Gradually stir in the milk, salt, and pepper. Cook until the mixture thickens, about 4-5 minutes. Reduce the heat to low and add the cheddar cheese, stirring continuously for about 2-3 minutes, until the cheese is completely melted. Remove from heat.

5 Pour the cooked macaroni into the cheese sauce and stir until the noodles are completely coated. Transfer the mixture to a lightly greased 4-quart baking dish and top generously with the prepared panko mixture and bacon. Bake for 20 minutes, or until the top is golden brown and the cheese is bubbling.

PASTA

ORECCHIETTE WITH TOMATO CREAM SAUCE

SERVES 4

This tomato sauce is like no other you've ever had. Good quality Italian sausage adds so much flavor to the sauce, while the cream cheese is an unusual way to add a rich creaminess. A picture of this recipe is featured on the cover of this book, and once you try it, you'll understand why.

INGREDIENTS

- 1 pound ground Italian sausage
- 1 (24-ounce) can tomato sauce
- 1 (14.5-ounce) can diced fire roasted tomatoes
- 1 tablespoon Italian seasoning
- 1 teaspoon garlic powder
- 1 teaspoon dried parsley
- 1 teaspoon salt
- ½ teaspoon pepper
- 1 (8-ounce) block cream cheese, cubed and softened
- ¼ cup parmesan cheese
- 1 (16-ounce) package orecchiette pasta

DIRECTIONS

1 Bring a large pot of water to a boil, add the pasta, and cook according to the package directions. Drain and set aside.

2 Meanwhile, in a large pan over medium-high heat, cook the sausage about 5-7 minutes, until browned. Remove from the pan and set aside.

3 Using the same pan, reduce the heat to medium and stir together the tomato sauce, diced tomatoes, Italian seasoning, garlic powder, parsley, salt, and pepper. Bring the sauce to a simmer and add in the cream cheese. Continue stirring for about 2-3 minutes, until combined. Return the Italian sausage and simmer for 4-5 minutes, watching carefully for bubbling. Stir in the parmesan cheese and remove from heat.

4 Add the cooked pasta to the sauce and stir until well combined. Serve topped with additional parmesan.

PASTA

MEATY MOZZARELLA PASTA BAKE

SERVES 4

You can take a simple pasta to the next level with a small extra step- just bake it topped with cheese! It may seem almost too easy, but we promise, it really does up the ante of this dish. We recommend using a good quality prepared sauce because it's a worthwhile shortcut for getting dinner done fast. It really doesn't get any easier than this!

INGREDIENTS

- 1 (16-ounce) package short pasta, such as cavatappi
- 1 pound ground beef
- 6 garlic cloves, minced
- 1 (24-ounce) jar marinara sauce
- 1½ teaspoons Italian seasoning
- 1 teaspoon chili powder
- ½ teaspoon salt
- ¼ teaspoon pepper
- 2 cups shredded mozzarella

DIRECTIONS

1 Bring a large pot of water to a boil, add the pasta, and cook according to the package directions. Drain and set aside.

2 Meanwhile, in a large pan over medium-high heat, cook the ground beef about 5-7 minutes, until browned. Add the garlic and cook for 30 seconds. Stir in the sauce, Italian seasoning, chili powder, salt, and pepper, cooking for 2 minutes. Add the pasta to the sauce and stir to combine.

3 Set the oven to broil on high. Transfer the mixture to a 9x9-inch baking dish, sprinkle with mozzarella and broil until the cheese is melted and bubbling, about 3-5 minutes.

Quick and Easy Meals

PASTA

SPAGHETTI AND MEATBALLS

SERVES 4

A true classic just made a bit easier! The meatballs simmer right in the sauce, making them so tender you won't even need a knife. We also eliminate the need to precook them, which gets you that much closer to dinner!

INGREDIENTS

- 1 pound ground beef
- 1 cup plain breadcrumbs
- ⅓ cup water
- 1 egg, beaten
- 1 tablespoon + ½ teaspoon dried oregano
- 1 teaspoon salt
- ¼ teaspoon pepper
- 3 tablespoons canola oil
- 2 garlic cloves, minced
- 1 (28-ounce) can tomato puree
- 1 (15-ounce) can diced tomatoes
- 3 tablespoons fresh chopped basil (4-6 leaves)
- 1 (16-ounce) package spaghetti noodles
- Grated parmesan cheese, for garnish

DIRECTIONS

1 In a large bowl, using clean hands, combine the beef, breadcrumbs, water, egg, 1 tablespoon of oregano, salt, and pepper. Gently form the mixture into 12 meatballs. Set aside.

2 In a large pot over medium heat, add the oil and minced garlic, cooking about 1-2 minutes, until fragrant, but not browned. Add the tomato puree, diced tomatoes, basil, and remaining ½ teaspoon of oregano. Bring the sauce to a boil, then reduce to a light simmer. Add the meatballs, cover, and cook about 10-15 minutes, until the meatballs are cooked through.

3 Meanwhile, bring a large pot of water to a boil, add the pasta, and cook according to the package directions. Drain and serve topped with sauce, meatballs, and grated parmesan.

PASTA

STROGANOFF MEATBALLS

SERVES 4

A "balls-y" twist on a dinner-time staple, these flavorful meatballs stand-in for the traditional sliced beef and are cooked right in the oven while you prepare the sauce and noodles. This alternative to pan-searing the meat means you'll get delicious results in less time and with much less effort.

INGREDIENTS

- ½ cup plain breadcrumbs
- ½ cup whole milk
- 1 teaspoon salt
- ½ teaspoon pepper
- 1 tablespoon canola oil
- 1 medium onion, diced
- 1 pound ground beef
- 1 pound button mushrooms, washed and halved
- 3 cups low-sodium beef broth
- 2 tablespoons Worcestershire sauce
- 1 tablespoon Dijon mustard
- 8 ounces egg noodles
- ⅓ cup sour cream
- ⅓ cup chopped fresh dill, divided

DIRECTIONS

1 Set oven to broil on high. In a large bowl, combine the breadcrumbs, milk, salt, and pepper, set aside.

2 In a large pot over medium-high heat, warm the oil. Add the onions and cook about 10 minutes, until softened and lightly browned. Remove from the heat and add ¼ cup of the cooked onions to the breadcrumb mixture. Add the ground beef, using clean hands, form the mixture into 1-inch balls. Place the balls on a rimmed baking sheet and broil for about 6-7 minutes, turning halfway through.

3 Meanwhile, adjust the heat to medium, add the mushrooms to the pot with the remaining onions and cook about 10 minutes, until the mushrooms have softened. Stir in the beef broth, Worcestershire sauce, and Dijon mustard, bringing the sauce to a boil. Stir in the noodles and add the cooked meatballs. Reduce the heat to medium-low and simmer for about 12 minutes, stirring occasionally, or until the noodles are fully cooked. Remove from the heat and stir in the sour cream and ¼ cup of the dill. Serve topped with remaining dill.

Quick and Easy Meals

PASTA

SPINACH & RICOTTA STUFFED SHELLS

SERVES 6

If you looked at this recipe and thought to yourself, "This sounds like lasagna," then you'd be right on the money! Using all the same ingredients, these shells taste just as good as lasagna but can be assembled quicker and cook much faster!

INGREDIENTS

- 1 (12-ounce) package jumbo shells
- 32 ounces ricotta cheese
- ¼ cup shredded parmesan
- 1 egg
- 4 garlic cloves, minced
- 2 cups baby spinach
- 1 (24-ounce) jar marinara sauce
- 2 cups mozzarella cheese

DIRECTIONS

1 Bring a large pot of water to a boil, add the pasta, and cook according to the package directions. Drain and set aside.

2 Preheat the oven to 350°F. In a large bowl, stir together the ricotta, parmesan, egg, garlic, and spinach until fully incorporated.

3 Prepare two 9x13-inch baking dishes by adding a ¼ cup of the marinara sauce to each dish, spreading evenly over the bottoms. When the shells are cool enough to handle, fill with about 2 tablespoons of the ricotta mixture each and place them into the prepared dishes. Repeat until all the shells are filled. Pour the remaining marinara over the filled shells and sprinkle 1 cup of mozzarella over each batch. Bake for 20 minutes, or until the cheese is fully melted and bubbling.

PASTA

SAUSAGE, SWEET POTATO, AND KALE PASTA

SERVES 4

This pasta dish is hearty, delicious, and it comes together fast! With ingredients like sweet potato and kale, it's the perfect nutrient-dense dinner for any day of the week.

INGREDIENTS

- 1 (8-ounce) package orecchiette pasta
- 2 large sweet potatoes, peeled and diced into 1-inch cubes
- 1 teaspoon, plus ½ teaspoon salt
- 1 tablespoon canola oil
- 1 large onion, diced
- 1 pound ground Italian sausage
- 6 garlic cloves, minced
- 4 cups kale, stems removed and chopped
- ½ cup grated parmesan
- ¼ teaspoon pepper

DIRECTIONS

1 Bring a large pot of water to a boil, add the pasta, and cook according to the package directions. Drain and set aside.

2 Meanwhile, in a large saucepan bring 5 cups of water to a boil. Add 1 teaspoon of salt and the sweet potatoes. Boil for about 10-12 minutes, or until the potatoes are tender. Drain and set aside.

3 In a large pan over medium-high heat, warm the oil. Add the onions and cook for about 6 minutes, or until the onions are lightly browned. Add the sausage and cook for 5-7 minutes, until browned. Add the garlic and cook for 30 seconds, until fragrant. Stir in the cooked sweet potatoes, cooking for 3 minutes. Add the kale and cover, allowing the kale to wilt, about 2-3 minutes. Stir in the pasta, parmesan, remaining salt, and pepper. Serve topped with parmesan.

Quick and Easy Meals

PASTA

TORTELLINI ALFREDO WITH BACON

SERVES 4

Any dinner where bacon, cheese, and pasta are present has to be good! This dish is loaded with comfort food favorites, tastes amazing, and fills you up without any regrets. Trust us, you won't want to miss out on this.

INGREDIENTS

- 19 ounces four cheese tortellini, fresh or frozen
- ½ cup butter
- 1 cup heavy cream
- 1½ cups + 1 tablespoon freshly grated parmesan
- ⅓ cup panko breadcrumbs
- 1 teaspoon canola oil
- 4 bacon slices, cooked and crumbled

DIRECTIONS

1 Bring water to a boil in a large pot. Add the tortellini and cook according to package directions. Drain and transfer to a broiler-safe 9x9-inch baking dish.

2 In a small saucepan over medium heat, melt the butter. Slowly add the heavy cream, stirring frequently until the mixture comes to a simmer. Turn the heat to low and continue stirring for 5 minutes. Remove the saucepan from the heat and stir in 1½ cups parmesan.

3 In a small bowl, stir together the breadcrumbs, 1 tablespoon parmesan, and oil. Set aside.

4 Pour the Alfredo sauce over the pasta, topping with the breadcrumb mixture and bacon. Set the oven to broil on high, place the dish in the oven for about 5 minutes, or until golden on top, watching carefully. Serve.

Quick and Easy Meals

RECIPES

Shredded Chicken Caesar Salad	81
Classic Cobb Salad with Creamy Garlic Dressing	83
Greek Salad	85
Chopped Kale Salad	87
Maurice Salad	89
Raspberry Quinoa Salad	91
Poached Salmon & Pecan Salad	93
Steak Fajita Salad	95
Thai Shrimp Salad	97
Tomato Beet Salad	99

There are so many varieties of salad out there. From those served on a bed of fresh leafy greens, to ones that skip the lettuce all together! This chapter explores the classics, and the more unique takes that will be new additions in your recipe rotation. We give you everything from tried-and-true recipes like Cobb and Maurice salads, and a homemade Caesar you won't believe is so easy to make. Let's not forget the exciting entrée salads like Thai Shrimp or Steak Fajita. You'll find so many flavors you know and love, offered up as lighter dinner alternatives. This chapter will prove that a salad is not just a salad; it can be a meal in itself, and equally satisfying.

SALADS

THAI SHRIMP SALAD PAGE 97

SALADS

SHREDDED CHICKEN CAESAR SALAD

SERVES 4

Invented in the 1920s, the Caesar salad is still very popular. Traditional Caesar dressing contains raw egg, but we made a slight tweak so you can have all of the flavor without the food safety worries! This recipe offers a great opportunity to use leftovers — whether it's chicken, shrimp, steak, or hard-boiled eggs, the options are endless.

INGREDIENTS

- 2 tablespoons mayo
- 2 teaspoons lemon juice
- 1 anchovy, finely minced into a paste, or 1 teaspoon anchovy paste
- ½ teaspoon Worcestershire sauce
- 1 garlic clove, minced
- ¼ teaspoon salt
- ¼ teaspoon pepper
- ¼ cup canola oil
- ¼ cup parmesan cheese
- 3 romaine hearts, chopped
- 2 cups cooked chicken breasts, shredded
- Croutons

DIRECTIONS

1 In a medium bowl, whisk together the mayo, lemon juice, anchovy, Worcestershire sauce, garlic, salt, and pepper. Slowly add the oil while stirring vigorously to combine; stir in the parmesan cheese to finish.

2 In a large bowl, toss together the romaine, chicken, and Caesar dressing. Serve with croutons on top.

SALADS

CLASSIC COBB SALAD WITH CREAMY GARLIC DRESSING

SERVES 4

When it comes to Cobb salads, there's lots of room to have fun with protein options and dressings. Our delicious, unique take on the classic features baby spinach, avocado, and colby jack cheese topped with a homemade creamy garlic dressing — which is similar to a Caesar dressing, but with a milder flavor that everyone will love.

DRESSING

- ¼ cup red wine vinegar
- 1 teaspoon lemon juice
- ¾ teaspoon Worcestershire sauce
- ¼ teaspoon sugar
- ¼ cup mayo
- 2 teaspoons salt
- 2 teaspoons Dijon mustard
- 1 garlic clove, minced
- ¾ teaspoon pepper
- ¾ cups canola oil

SALAD

- 1 head romaine lettuce, shredded or chopped
- 2 cups baby spinach
- 2 medium tomatoes, chopped
- 6 bacon slices, cooked and crumbled
- 2 cooked chicken breasts, shredded or cut into ¼-inch chunks
- 3 hard-boiled eggs, chopped
- 1 avocado, chopped
- ½ cup shredded colby jack cheese

DIRECTIONS

1 In a medium bowl, whisk together the red wine vinegar, lemon juice, Worcestershire sauce, and sugar, until the sugar dissolves. Add the mayo, salt, Dijon mustard, garlic, and pepper. Slowly add the oil, whisking until combined and thickened.

2 In a large bowl, toss together the romaine and spinach. Arrange the tomatoes, bacon, chicken, eggs, avocado, and cheese on the top. Toss before serving with dressing on the side.

Quick and Easy Meals

SALADS

GREEK SALAD

SERVES 4

You may be looking at this recipe and scratching your head asking, "Where's the lettuce?". Certainly, you can add it, but this salad is so delicious and satisfying, you probably won't feel the need to!

VINAIGRETTE

- ⅔ cup canola oil
- ⅓ cup red wine vinegar
- ½ lemon, juiced
- 1 green onion, white parts only
- 5 Kalamata olives, pitted
- 1 teaspoon dried oregano
- 1 teaspoon salt
- ½ teaspoon pepper

SALAD

- 2 large English cucumbers, diced
- 2 large bell peppers, diced
- 1 (16-ounce) jar pickled beets, diced
- 3 green onions, sliced
- 1 large tomato, diced
- ¾ cup feta cheese
- ¾ cup Kalamata pitted olives

DIRECTIONS

1 In a blender, add the oil, red wine vinegar, lemon juice, green onion, olives, oregano, salt, and pepper. Pulse until well mixed.

2 In a large bowl, combine the cucumbers, peppers, beets, onions, and tomatoes.

3 Serve tossed with the dressing and topped with feta and olives.

SALADS

CHOPPED KALE SALAD

SERVES 4

Kale is either praised for being society's beacon of health or hated for its tough leaves and bitter flavor. Wherever your personal feelings may land on that spectrum, we challenge you to give this salad a try! Baby kale — which requires less preparation and typically has more tender, mildly flavored leaves — can be used as well.

DRESSING

- 3 tablespoons canola oil
- 2 tablespoons apple cider vinegar
- 2 tablespoons lemon juice
- 2 garlic cloves, minced
- 3 basil leaves, minced
- ¼ teaspoon cayenne pepper

SALAD

- 4 cups kale, stems removed and chopped
- 1 red pepper, chopped
- ½ cup cooked quinoa, cooled
- 1 small red onion, sliced
- ¼ cup tomatoes, chopped
- 4 tablespoons nutritional yeast or parmesan
- 3 tablespoons hemp seeds

DIRECTIONS

1 In a small bowl, stir together the oil, vinegar, lemon juice, garlic, basil, and cayenne pepper.

2 In a large bowl, toss together the kale, red pepper, quinoa, red onion, tomatoes, and nutritional yeast or parmesan. Top with hemp seeds and serve with dressing on the side.

Quick and Easy Meals

SALADS

MAURICE SALAD

SERVES 4

Popularized in Detroit, MI, by the J.L. Hudson department store, this salad continues to be served in many American restaurants. Once you try it, you won't be surprised as to why. The homemade dressing is zesty, creamy, and fresh. Not to mention the abundance of protein this salad packs with the ham, turkey, cheese, and egg. This salad is worthy of being called a meal in itself.

DRESSING

- 2 tablespoons vinegar
- 1½ teaspoon lemon juice
- 1½ teaspoons sugar
- 1½ teaspoons Dijon mustard
- 1 cup mayo
- 1 hard-boiled egg, finely diced
- 2 tablespoons chopped fresh parsley
- ½ teaspoon salt
- ⅛ teaspoon pepper

SALAD

- 1 head iceberg lettuce, chopped or shredded
- 1 pound ham, cubed
- 1 pound turkey breasts, cubed
- 1 pound swiss cheese, cubed
- ½ cup slivered sweet gherkins pickles (sweet relish, rinsed in a strainer, can be substituted)
- 12 green olives stuffed with pimento, for garnish
- 2 hard-boiled eggs, cut in half

DIRECTIONS

1 In a medium bowl, whisk together the vinegar, lemon juice, sugar, and Dijon, until the sugar dissolves. Add the mayo, diced egg, parsley, salt, and pepper. Continue whisking until fully incorporated.

2 Arrange a bed of lettuce on each plate. Place ¼ pound of ham, turkey, and swiss on each plate. Divide the pickles evenly over each serving. Garnish each salad with 4 olives and an egg half.

RASPBERRY QUINOA SALAD

SERVES 4

Everyone needs a break from heavy foods, and what better way to cleanse your palate than with this fresh, simple salad? Pecans and chia seeds ensure that even the biggest appetites will be satisfied, while the raspberries add a fresh sweetness to the dish.

DRESSING

- 3 tablespoons canola oil
- 1 tablespoon red wine vinegar
- 1 teaspoon salt
- 1 teaspoon sugar or honey
- 1 teaspoon dried oregano
- ¼ teaspoon Dijon mustard
- ⅛ teaspoon pepper

SALAD

- 1 bunch kale, stems removed and chopped
- 1 romaine heart, chopped
- ⅔ cup cooked quinoa
- 1 small cucumber, chopped
- ¼ cup chopped pecans
- 1 teaspoon chia seeds
- 3 ounces raspberries

DIRECTIONS

1 In a small bowl, whisk together the oil, vinegar, salt, sugar or honey, oregano, Dijon mustard, and pepper. Set aside.

2 In a large bowl, toss together the kale, romaine, quinoa, cucumber, pecans, chia seeds, and raspberries. Serve with dressing on the side.

SALADS

POACHED SALMON & PECAN SALAD

SERVES 4

Tangy honey mustard dressing, sweet roasted pecans, and protein-packed poached salmon come together to make an entree salad that truly stands out. Served on a bed of peppery arugula, this salad has the perfect balance of flavors.

SWEET ROASTED NUTS

- 2 tablespoons brown sugar
- 2 teaspoons sugar
- 2 teaspoons vanilla extract
- 1 cup chopped pecans

DRESSING

- ¼ cup Dijon mustard
- ¼ cup honey
- ¼ cup canola oil
- 1 teaspoon salt
- ¼ teaspoon pepper

SALAD

- 4 (4-ounce) salmon fillets
- 1 lemon, juiced
- 3 green onions, quartered
- 2 teaspoon black peppercorns
- 2 teaspoons salt
- 10 ounces baby arugula
- 10 ounces spring mix
- ⅔ cup radishes, diced

DIRECTIONS

1 In a small nonstick pan over medium heat, add the brown sugar, sugar, vanilla extract, and pecans, cooking for 15-30 seconds, just enough for the sugar to melt. Once the sugar melts, stir until the pecans are coated, then transfer them to a plate in a single layer to cool.

2 In a small bowl, stir together the Dijon, honey, oil, salt, and pepper. Set aside.

3 In a large pan, add the salmon fillets and cover with cold water; add lemon juice, green onions, peppercorns, and salt. Over medium-high heat, bring the liquid to a simmer, turn the fillets, remove skillet from heat, and let stand covered for 7 minutes. Remove the fillets from the poaching liquid and transfer to a plate to cool for 5 minutes. Using two forks, flake the salmon off the skin into small pieces.

4 In a large bowl, toss together the arugula, spring mix, radishes, roasted nuts, and flaked salmon. Top with the dressing and serve.

SALADS

STEAK FAJITA SALAD

SERVES 4

Perfectly seasoned steak on a bed of garden-fresh vegetables and lettuce are the makings of a delicious meal. This salad has the robust flavors of the sizzling skillets you see at many Tex-Mex restaurants, but with fewer carbs!

MARINADE

- ¼ cup low-sodium soy sauce
- ¼ cup Worcestershire sauce
- 2 tablespoons canola oil
- 2 garlic cloves, minced
- 1 teaspoon cumin
- 1 teaspoon salt
- ½ teaspoon pepper

SALAD

- 1 teaspoon canola oil
- 2 (6-ounce) sirloin fillets
- 1 (10-ounce) bag mixed salad greens
- 2 cups grape or cherry tomatoes, halved
- 1 medium red onion, diced
- 1 large green bell pepper, chopped
- 1 large red bell pepper, chopped
- ½ cup whole kernel yellow corn, drained and rinsed
- ½ cup dark red kidney beans, drained and rinsed
- Tri-colored tortilla strips
- Shredded cheddar jack cheese, for garnish
- 2 cups Italian dressing

DIRECTIONS

1 In a small bowl, whisk together the soy sauce, Worcestershire, oil, garlic, cumin, salt, and pepper. In a large resealable bag, add the marinade and sirloin fillets, marinating for 15 minutes.

2 In a large pan or grill pan over medium-high heat, warm the oil. Add the steaks and cook about 5-6 minutes per side, until the outside is browned. Remove from pan and rest for 3 minutes before slicing. Slice against the grain into ¼-inch strips.

3 On a large platter, arrange the salad greens, topping with tomatoes, onion, green pepper, red pepper, corn, and beans. Add the sliced steak on top and garnish with tortilla strips and cheese. Serve with dressing on the side.

Quick and Easy Meals

SALADS

THAI SHRIMP SALAD

SERVES 6

This delicious Asian-inspired salad has a little bit of kick, a little bit of sweet, and a whole lot of flavor! It comes together quickly because you don't have to cook anything. That makes this the perfect meal on the nights when you just don't feel like cooking!

PEANUT DRESSING

- ⅓ cup hoisin sauce
- ⅓ cup rice wine vinegar
- ¼ cup peanut butter
- 2 tablespoons sesame oil
- 1 tablespoon brown sugar
- 2½ teaspoons grated fresh ginger
- 2 teaspoons Sriracha

SALAD MIX

- 5 cups romaine lettuce, shredded
- 5 cups shredded Napa cabbage
- 1 cup shredded carrots
- 1 cup frozen edamame (soybeans), thawed
- 1 bunch green onions, chopped
- ½ cup chopped fresh cilantro
- 1 (8-ounce) can sliced water chestnuts
- ½ cup sliced almonds
- 1 pound frozen cooked shrimp, thawed
- 2 tablespoons black or white sesame seeds
- ¾ cup crispy wonton strips

DIRECTIONS

1 In a small bowl, stir together the hoisin, rice wine vinegar, peanut butter, sesame oil, brown sugar, ginger, and hot chile paste. Set aside.

2 In a large bowl, toss together the romaine, cabbage, carrots, edamame, green onions, cilantro, water chestnuts, almonds, and shrimp.

3 Serve topped with dressing, sesame seeds, and wonton strips.

SALADS

TOMATO BEET SALAD

SERVES 4

Not only is this recipe stunning, but it's also incredibly simple. Its inspiration comes from the Italian Caprese salad mixed with a traditional Greek salad. Fresh vegetables, pickled beets, balsamic, and deliciously salty feta cheese really makes this salad something special!

INGREDIENTS

- 3 large heirloom tomatoes, sliced
- 2 cups small heirloom tomatoes, halved
- 2 (15-ounce) jars sliced pickled beets
- ½ cup crumbled feta cheese
- ⅓ cup sliced fresh basil
- 1 green onion, thinly sliced
- ¼ cup balsamic vinegar

DIRECTIONS

1 On a large platter, arrange the tomatoes and beets as desired. Top with feta, basil, and onion; drizzle with balsamic vinegar.

Quick and Easy Meals

RECIPES

Creole Shrimp Pasta	**103**
Fish and Chips	**105**
Garlic and Parmesan Salmon	**107**
Lemon and Herb Butter Salmon	**109**
Dijon Salmon	**111**
Seasoned Whitefish with Sun-Dried Tomatoes & Spinach	**113**
Shrimp Scampi with Angel Hair	**115**
Shrimp with Bacon & Cheesy Grits	**117**

Folks seem to either love or hate seafood, but the fact of the matter is, it's packed with protein and is incredibly lean. This chapter will reignite the flame for those who already love seafood and are looking for new recipes, and to hopefully convert those who may be on the fence but want to incorporate fish into their routine. From shrimp to whitefish to salmon, we found inspiration from the bottom of the ocean all the way to the top. We have packed this chapter full of must-try recipes you may have never heard of, along with reworked versions of classics you'll definitely recognize. You can look forward to Shrimp with Bacon and Cheesy Grits, Lemon and Herb Butter Salmon, and fish and chips, just to name a few. The task of making seafood at home is no longer daunting with these easy recipes.

SEAFOOD

SHRIMP WITH BACON & CHEESY GRITS PAGE 117

SEAFOOD

CREOLE SHRIMP PASTA

SERVES 4

With the perfect blend of kick and creaminess, this dish brings just the right amount of heat to your plate without being too hot. So, if you're not the type of person to test your heat limits, fear not! Topped with succulent shrimp, this dish is sure to awaken your taste buds!

SEASONING

- ¼ teaspoon smoked paprika
- ¼ teaspoon onion powder
- ¼ teaspoon garlic powder
- ¼ teaspoon cayenne pepper
- ¼ teaspoon dried thyme
- ¼ teaspoon dried oregano
- ¼ teaspoon dried parsley
- ¼ teaspoon black pepper

INGREDIENTS

- 1 pound penne pasta
- 1 pound large shrimp, peeled and deveined
- ½ cup butter
- ¼ cup flour
- 2 cups half & half
- 1 cup grated parmesan cheese
- ½ teaspoon garlic powder
- 1 teaspoon canola oil

DIRECTIONS

1 In a small bowl, stir together the paprika, onion powder, garlic powder, cayenne pepper, thyme, oregano, parsley, and pepper. Set aside.

2 Bring a large pot of water to a boil, add the pasta, and cook according to the package directions. Drain and set aside.

3 Meanwhile, in a small saucepan over medium heat, melt the butter and whisk in the flour, stirring constantly about 2-4 minutes, until smooth and it turns a peanut butter color. Slowly add the half & half, stirring constantly. Increase the heat to medium and continue stirring for 4 minutes, until the sauce is thickened. Stir in the parmesan cheese and garlic powder. Reduce heat to low, stirring occasionally for about 4 minutes until smooth.

4 Add the noodles back into the pot, along with half of the seasoning mixture, and lightly toss. Sprinkle the remaining seasoning over both sides of the shrimp.

5 In a large pan over medium heat, warm the oil. Add the shrimp and cook the shrimp for 3 minutes on each side. Add the shrimp and sauce to the pasta and toss to combine.

Quick and Easy Meals

SEAFOOD

FISH AND CHIPS

SERVES 4

Whether you're looking to be more health-conscious or just don't like the idea of cooking with hot oil, you'll love that we eliminated the hassle of deep-frying this dinnertime staple. The fish turns out crispy and perfectly flaky, right in your oven. The potato wedges cook right alongside the fish, making this recipe as simple as can be!

INGREDIENTS

- 2 cups panko breadcrumbs
- 4 medium russet potatoes, scrubbed, cut into ¼-inch wedges, and dried
- ¼ cup canola oil
- 1 teaspoon salt, divided
- 1 teaspoon paprika, divided
- ½ teaspoon pepper, divided
- 2 eggs, beaten
- ½ cup flour
- 1½ pounds skinless, boneless haddock or cod fillets, patted dry, cut in 4-ounce fillets
- 1 teaspoon seafood seasoning, such as Old Bay®

TARTAR SAUCE

- ½ cup mayo
- 2 tablespoons sweet relish
- ¼ teaspoon onion powder
- ¼ teaspoon dried dill
- 1 teaspoon lemon juice
- Salt, to taste

DIRECTIONS

1 Preheat the oven to 425°F. On a baking sheet, spread the breadcrumbs in a thin layer, and toast in the oven until golden brown, about 4-6 minutes. Remove from the oven and set aside to cool.

2 Meanwhile, in a small bowl, stir together the mayo, relish, onion powder, dill, lemon juice, and salt. Refrigerate until ready to serve.

3 Add the potato wedges to another baking sheet. Drizzle with the oil, and sprinkle evenly with ½ teaspoon salt, ½ teaspoon paprika, and ¼ teaspoon pepper, tossing well to coat. Bake on the lower rack for 30 minutes, flipping halfway through.

4 Meanwhile, place the toasted panko in a shallow bowl. In another shallow bowl, beat the eggs. In a large resealable bag, combine the flour, remaining salt, and pepper. Season the fish with the remaining paprika and seafood seasoning.

5 Working with two fillets a time, add the fish to the flour bag, closing and shaking to fully coat. Remove the fish from the bag, shaking off the excess flour. Dip each filet into the egg on both sides, then place into the breadcrumb mixture, pressing gently to make sure they stick. Gently shake off any excess crumbs, and place on a parchment-lined baking sheet.

6 Cook on the upper rack for 15 minutes. Serve fish with homemade chips and sauce.

SEAFOOD

GARLIC AND PARMESAN SALMON

SERVES 4

If your salmon routine is getting boring and repetitive, give it an Italian-inspired upgrade! With its savory Parmesan crust, this salmon is literally coated in flavor. Serve it as is, or over a salad for a perfect dinner.

INGREDIENTS

- 4 (6-ounce) salmon fillets
- 3 tablespoons canola oil
- 1 teaspoon salt
- ½ teaspoon pepper
- 4 garlic cloves, minced
- 1 cup grated parmesan cheese
- ¼ cup fresh parsley, chopped

DIRECTIONS

1 Preheat the oven to 400°F. Line a baking sheet with parchment paper.

2 Pat the salmon dry, brush with the oil on all sides, and season with salt and pepper. Place the salmon skin-side down on the parchment, spread garlic on top, then sprinkle with parmesan and chopped parsley. Bake for 15-20 minutes. Set the oven to broil on high. Broil for 2-3 minutes, until the cheese is browned, watching closely. Serve.

SEAFOOD
LEMON AND HERB BUTTER SALMON

SERVES 6

Bathed in a melted butter sauce, this salmon turns out flavorful and moist. Baking in a parchment-lined foil package ensures that all of the flavor is locked in and that the salmon is tender.

INGREDIENTS

- 1/3 cup butter
- 2 tablespoons lemon juice
- 6 garlic cloves, minced
- 1/2 teaspoon salt
- 1/4 teaspoon pepper
- 2 tablespoons fresh parsley, chopped
- 2 pounds salmon filet
- 2 lemons, sliced

DIRECTIONS

1 Preheat the oven to 375°F. Line a baking sheet with a large sheet of aluminum foil (large enough to seal the salmon in) and parchment paper; set aside.

2 In a small saucepan over medium-low heat, melt the butter. Stir in the lemon juice, garlic, salt, pepper, and parsley, cooking for about 2 minutes until fragrant, and remove from the heat. Lay the salmon on the baking sheet, brush with butter sauce, top with lemon slices, then close foil around the salmon and bake for 15-20 minutes.

3 Remove from the oven. If desired, carefully open the package and broil on high for 2-3 minutes, watching carefully to ensure the parchment doesn't burn. Serve.

SEAFOOD

DIJON SALMON

SERVES 6

This refreshing twist on salmon is served with tender asparagus and topped with a mildly tangy sauce. Cooked in individual parchment packets makes for a fun presentation and a delicate way to steam cook your dinner.

INGREDIENTS

- 2 pounds salmon, cut into 6 fillets
- 3 tablespoons finely chopped parsley
- 2 garlic cloves, minced
- 2 tablespoons Dijon mustard
- ½ teaspoon salt
- ¼ teaspoon pepper
- 2 tablespoons lemon juice
- 1 bundle asparagus, rinsed and cut into 2-inch pieces
- 2 tablespoons canola oil

DIRECTIONS

1 Preheat the oven to 450°F. Cut the parchment paper into 6 large pieces. In a small bowl, stir together the parsley, garlic, Dijon, salt, pepper, and lemon juice.

2 Evenly distribute the asparagus on the parchment pieces and drizzle with oil. Place salmon fillets on each pile of asparagus and brush with mustard mixture. Fold the parchment closed over the salmon and asparagus to create a packet, stapling to keep closed, if necessary. Place the packets on a rimmed baking sheet and bake for 12-15 minutes. Carefully remove from the oven and let rest for 5 minutes before opening and serving.

SEAFOOD

SEASONED WHITEFISH WITH SUN-DRIED TOMATOES & SPINACH

SERVES 4

Seasoned whitefish provides protein, while spinach is rich in vitamins and minerals — and the whole dish gets a flavor boost from the sundried tomatoes. Simple to prepare and cook, it's a perfect busy weeknight meal. Best of all, this dinner is absolutely delicious!

INGREDIENTS

- 1 teaspoon canola oil
- 2 garlic cloves, minced
- 4 (4-ounce) cod fillets or other whitefish
- ¼ teaspoon salt
- ¼ teaspoon pepper
- ¼ teaspoon cayenne
- ¼ teaspoon paprika
- 10 ounces fresh spinach
- ¼ cup chopped sun-dried tomatoes packed in oil, drained
- 2 tablespoons sun-dried tomato oil, reserved from tomatoes

DIRECTIONS

1 Season both sides of the fish with salt, pepper, cayenne, and paprika. In a large pan over medium heat, warm the oil. Add the garlic and cook about 1 minute, until it begins to brown. Carefully add the fish to the pan. Cover and cook about 8-10 minutes, until the fish flakes easily with a fork. Remove the fish, cover, and set aside.

2 Add the spinach and sun-dried tomatoes to the pan, cover and cook about 1-2 minutes, or until the spinach is just wilted. Place the spinach and tomatoes on a serving plate, topping with the fish. Finish each portion with a drizzle of oil from the pan.

SEAFOOD

SHRIMP SCAMPI WITH ANGEL HAIR

SERVES 4

Traditionally, Shrimp Scampi is made with a combination of butter, garlic, and dry white wine; it is most commonly served with pasta, as we've done here, but is sometimes served with bread or on its own. We have brightened our version up a little bit by adding lemon juice, giving this a fresh and light feel.

INGREDIENTS

- 1 (16-ounce) box angel hair pasta
- 2 tablespoons canola oil
- 1 pound large shrimp, peeled and deveined, thawed if frozen
- 8 tablespoons butter
- 3 garlic cloves, minced
- ⅓ cup vermouth or white wine
- ¼ cup lemon juice
- ½ teaspoon salt
- ¼ teaspoon pepper
- 2 tablespoons chopped fresh parsley

DIRECTIONS

1 Bring a large pot of water to a boil, add the pasta, and cook according to the package directions. Drain and set aside.

2 Meanwhile, in a large pan over medium-high heat, warm the oil. Add the shrimp and cook until pink, about 3 minutes per side; transfer to a bowl, cover, and set aside.

3 In the same pan, reduce the heat to medium, add the butter and allow to melt. Add the garlic and cook about 1-2 minutes, until fragrant. Add the vermouth or wine, lemon juice, salt, and pepper, cooking an additional 2 minutes. Remove from heat, stir in parsley, then add pasta and shrimp, tossing to coat.

Quick and Easy Meals

SEAFOOD

SHRIMP WITH BACON & CHEESY GRITS

SERVES 4

Cheesy, bacon-y (we know that's not a word), and loaded with shrimp, there's a flavor-loaded dinner ahead of you! We know eating grits for dinner isn't in the norm for most, but if this is something new to you, you won't be disappointed. When paired with a protein, grits make a satisfying meal for all.

INGREDIENTS

- 5 slices thick-cut bacon, diced
- 2 tablespoons butter
- 1 pound large fresh shrimp
- 1 teaspoon seafood seasoning, such as Old Bay®
- 1 green onion, chopped and divided
- 4 cups buttermilk
- 1 cup quick cooking grits
- ½ cup shredded mild cheddar cheese

DIRECTIONS

1 In a large skillet over medium-high heat, cook the bacon about 5-7 minutes, until crispy. Remove bacon and place on paper towels. Set aside. Drain the bacon grease, leaving about 1 tablespoon in the pan, and add the butter. Add the shrimp, seafood seasoning, and half of the green onions, cooking for about 3 minutes, until shrimp are cooked through. Crumble bacon and add to skillet. Remove from heat and cover.

2 In a medium saucepan over medium-low heat, add the buttermilk and cook about 4-5 minutes, until it reaches a simmer. Gently stir in the grits, cover, and cook for 5-7 minutes. Remove the grits from heat and stir in cheese. **3** Serve shrimp and bacon over the grits.

Quick and Easy Meals

RECIPES

Classic Beef Tacos	**121**
Chicken Quesadillas	**123**
Steak Fajitas	**125**
Green Chili Chicken Enchilada Casserole	**127**
Skirt Steak Tacos	**129**
Stuffed Poblano Peppers	**131**
Tex Mex Skillet	**133**
Tex Mex Stuffed Peppers	**135**

Exploring new flavors and cuisines is fun all on its own, and to us, it's even more fun when you can try them right at home! This chapter explores a mixture of various Mexican and Tex Mex inspired flavors, bringing a little spice and flair to your plate. From Quesadillas to an Enchilada Casserole, Stuffed Poblanos to Steak Fajitas, these flavor-filled recipes are sure to impress. Check out how easy these recipes are to make and how quickly they come together!

TEX MEX

TEX MEX STUFFED PEPPERS PAGE 135

TEX MEX

CLASSIC BEEF TACOS

YIELD 12 | SERVES 4

While we all know what tacos are and how they're supposed to taste, when was the last time you made some without using a seasoning packet? Making beef tacos from scratch is barely any extra effort, and the flavors are next-level. Give these a try on your next taco Tuesday and see what fresh flavors await you!

INGREDIENTS

- 1 teaspoon canola oil
- 1 medium onion, minced
- 3 garlic cloves, minced
- 1½ pounds ground beef
- 4 teaspoons chili powder
- ¼ teaspoon cayenne pepper
- 1 teaspoon cumin
- 1 teaspoon salt
- ½ teaspoon pepper
- ½ cup tomato paste
- 12 soft tortillas or hard taco shells

TOPPINGS

- Lime wedges
- Shredded lettuce
- Diced tomato
- Shredded cheese
- Green onion

DIRECTIONS

1 In a large pan over medium-high heat, warm the oil. Add the onions and cook about 10-12 minutes, until lightly browned. Add the garlic and beef, cooking about 7-9 minutes, until meat is no longer pink. Add chili powder, cayenne, cumin, salt, pepper, and tomato paste, stirring to combine, cooking for 3-5 minutes.

2 Serve in tortillas or taco shells and top with desired toppings.

Quick and Easy Meals

TEX MEX

CHICKEN QUESADILLAS

SERVES 4

Chicken quesadillas are a simple and satisfying way to change up your chicken routine. Loaded with cheese, bacon, and black beans, this version kicks it up a notch! Serve it with some sour cream or salsa, and you've got dinner! Using leftover chicken makes this dinner a great "use it up" option.

INGREDIENTS

- 4 (4-ounce) boneless skinless chicken breasts, tenderized to ¼-inch thickness
- 2 tablespoons canola oil, divided
- 2 tablespoons lemon juice
- ¼ teaspoon onion powder
- ¼ teaspoon garlic powder
- ¼ teaspoon chili powder
- 1 teaspoon salt
- ½ teaspoon pepper
- 1 small onion, diced
- 1 red pepper, diced
- 8 (6-inch) flour tortillas
- 4 bacon slices, cooked and crumbled
- 3 cups shredded colby jack cheese
- 1 (15.5-ounce) can sweet corn, drained
- 1 (15.5-ounce) can black beans, drained

TOPPINGS

Guacamole
Salsa
Sour cream

DIRECTIONS

1 In a medium bowl or plastic bag, combine the chicken, 1 tablespoon oil, lemon juice, onion powder, garlic powder, chili powder, salt, and pepper, making sure chicken is fully coated.

2 In a large pan over medium-high heat, warm the remaining oil. Add the chicken and cook 6-8 minutes per side, until cooked through. Remove chicken and set aside. Using the same pan, add the onions and red pepper, cooking for about 10 minutes, until the onions are starting to brown. Remove from pan and set aside. Cut chicken into ½-inch cubes.

3 Using the same pan, wipe it clean with a paper towel. Reduce the heat to medium-low, lay 1 tortilla in the pan, layering with ¼ cup of cheese, 4 ounces of chicken, 1 tablespoon of bacon, ½ cup of corn, ½ cup of beans, ¼ of the onion and pepper mixture, and finish with a ¼ cup more of the cheese, topping with another tortilla. Heat for 3-4 minutes, until the cheese has melted, carefully flip and cook another 3-4 minutes. Repeat with remaining quesadillas. Cut each quesadilla into 6 pieces, and serve with guacamole, salsa, or sour cream.

TEX MEX

STEAK FAJITAS

SERVES 4

Who can resist the sizzling fajitas at Tex-Mex style restaurants? Besides the firey presentation, the aroma alone is enough to get anyone salivating! We wanted to turn one of our restaurant favorites into an easy at-home meal. Marinated steak paired with caramelized onions and tender peppers, load them up with all of your favorite toppings, and enjoy!

INGREDIENTS

- 3 tablespoons canola oil, divided
- 3 limes, zested and juiced, divided
- 1 tablespoon paprika
- 2 teaspoons packed brown sugar
- 1 teaspoon cumin
- 1½ teaspoons chili powder
- ½ teaspoon garlic powder
- 1 teaspoon salt
- 1½ pounds sirloin steaks
- 1 large onion, thinly sliced
- 1 red bell pepper, sliced
- 1 green bell pepper, sliced
- 12 (6-inch) flour tortillas

TOPPINGS

Shredded cheddar cheese
Shredded lettuce
Sour cream
Guacamole

DIRECTIONS

1 In a medium bowl, combine 1 tablespoon of oil, a ¼ cup of the lime juice, lime zest, paprika, brown sugar, cumin, chili powder, garlic powder, and salt, stirring until sugar is dissolved. Submerge the steak in the marinade. Set aside.

2 Meanwhile, in a large pan over medium-high heat, warm the remaining oil. Add the onions, cooking about 10-12 minutes, until the onions start to brown, add the peppers and continue to cook about 8-10 minutes, until the peppers have softened. Remove from the pan and set aside. Increase heat to medium-high, add the steak to the pan, cooking about 2-3 minutes per side, until browned on the outside. Remove from pan and let sit about 5 minutes, then cut across the grain into thin slices.

3 Return the meat and peppers back into the pan over medium heat and toss together for about 3 minutes, until everything is heated through.

4 Serve in the tortillas, paired with the toppings of choice.

TEX MEX

GREEN CHILI CHICKEN ENCHILADA CASSEROLE

SERVES 6

Enchiladas are delicious, but we know they can be a bit time consuming to prepare. We removed our least favorite part, the rolling. By layering it like lasagna, we cut down on the prep time, so it's from oven to table in 30 minutes. What's not to love about that?

INGREDIENTS

1	pound cooked shredded chicken thighs
¼	cup sour cream
4	ounces cream cheese
1	teaspoon garlic powder
1	teaspoon salt
½	teaspoon onion powder
1	(10-ounce) can green enchilada sauce
18	corn tortillas
3	(4-ounce) cans chopped green chilies
4	cups shredded colby jack cheese

DIRECTIONS

1 Preheat the oven to 350°F.

2 In a large bowl, stir together the shredded chicken, sour cream, cream cheese, garlic powder, salt, and onion powder until fully combined.

3 Pour a thin layer of enchilada sauce into a 9x13-inch pan, using just enough to coat the bottom. Layer ⅓ of the tortillas on the bottom of the pan, cover tortillas evenly with ½ of the chicken mixture, add 1 can of green chilies, pour ⅓ of the enchilada sauce over the chilies, and sprinkle with ⅓ of the cheese and repeat. Layer the last of the tortillas on the top, finishing with remaining sauce and chilies, and cover with cheese.

4 Cover with foil and bake for 15 minutes. Remove the foil and cook another 5 minutes, until the cheese is melted, bubbling, and browned. Let rest for 5 minutes before serving.

TEX MEX

SKIRT STEAK TACOS

SERVES 4

While we love steak, we'd be lying if we said that was the main attraction of these tacos. It's really the charred vegetable salsa that stands out here, adding a delicious, slightly smoky flavor. These couldn't be easier to make, and you don't even need to get the grill out for it!

SALSA

- 1½ cups corn, fresh, canned, or frozen and thawed
- 8 ounces grape tomatoes
- 1 bunch green onions, cut into 2-inch pieces
- 2 tablespoons canola oil, divided
- ½ small jicama, peeled and diced
- 1 small lime, juiced
- ½ teaspoon salt
- ¼ teaspoon sugar

STEAK

- 1 pound skirt steak, cut into 4 steaks, trimmed of fat
- ½ teaspoon onion powder
- ½ teaspoon garlic powder
- 1 teaspoon salt
- ½ teaspoon pepper
- ½ teaspoon chili powder
- 8 (6-inch) flour tortillas, warmed

DIRECTIONS

1 Set the oven to broil on high. On a rimmed baking sheet, add the corn, tomatoes, and green onions. Toss with 1 tablespoon of the oil. Cook for 12-15 minutes, stirring every 2 minutes until the vegetables start to char and the tomatoes have burst. Remove from the oven and transfer to a medium bowl. Add the jicama, lime juice, salt, and sugar, stirring until well coated.

2 Season both sides of the steaks with the onion powder, garlic powder, salt, pepper, and chili powder. In a large skillet over medium-high heat, warm the remaining oil. Add the steaks and cook for 2-3 minutes per side, until browned. Transfer to a plate, cover with foil, and let rest for 5 minutes.

3 Slice the steak into thin strips, cutting across the grain. Serve on a warmed tortilla topped with the prepared salsa.

Quick and Easy Meals

TEX MEX

STUFFED POBLANO PEPPERS

SERVES 4

Have you ever tried a stuffed poblano pepper? Similar to a regular stuffed pepper, but these come with a kick. Filled to the brim with chorizo, rice, onions, and so much more, they're a fun twist on the classic that will make eating them new and exciting!

INGREDIENTS

- 1 pound chorizo sausage
- ½ cup cooked rice
- 1 small onion, finely diced
- ½ cup taco sauce, divided
- ¼ cup shredded cheddar cheese
- 1 teaspoon cumin
- 2 poblano peppers, halved lengthwise and seeds removed
- ¼ cup water

TOPPINGS

- Sour cream
- Shredded lettuce
- Salsa
- Shredded cheese

DIRECTIONS

1 Preheat the oven to 350°F. In a large pan over medium-high heat, add the chorizo, stirring for about 10 minutes, until completely browned and broken into small pieces. Remove the pan from the heat, stir in the rice, onion, ¼ cup of the taco sauce, cheese, and cumin until fully combined. Fill halved poblano peppers with the chorizo mixture and place in a 9x13-inch baking dish. Drizzle 1 tablespoon of taco sauce over each pepper.

2 Pour the water into the bottom of the baking dish and cover loosely with foil. Bake for 30-45 minutes, until the peppers reach desired tenderness. Remove from the oven and allow to sit for 5 minutes before serving. Serve with sour cream, lettuce, salsa, or toppings of choice!

TEX MEX SKILLET

SERVES 4

One-pot meals are not only convenient, but they're also a fun way to serve dinner. This Tex Mex skillet has all of your favorite flavors loaded up right in front of you! Serve it with tortillas, and dinner is ready!

INGREDIENTS

- 1 teaspoon canola oil
- 1 small onion, chopped
- 3 garlic cloves, minced
- 1 pound ground beef
- 2 tablespoons chili powder
- 1 teaspoon cumin
- ¾ teaspoon salt
- 1½ cups cooked white rice
- 1 (14.5-ounce) can black beans, drained and rinsed
- 2 (10-ounce) cans Mexican stewed tomatoes
- 1 cup shredded sharp cheddar cheese
- 8-12 (6-inch) flour tortillas

DIRECTIONS

1 Preheat the oven to 350°F. In a skillet over medium heat, warm the oil. Add the onions and garlic, cooking for 3 minutes, stirring occasionally. Add the beef and cook about 10 minutes, until completely browned; drain if needed. Stir in the chili powder, cumin, salt, rice, beans, and tomatoes. Continue cooking for 5 minutes, stirring occasionally, until heated through.

2 Sprinkle with cheese and place in the oven, cooking about 15 minutes, until the cheese has melted. Remove from the oven and rest for 10 minutes. Serve in or with tortillas.

TEX MEX STUFFED PEPPERS

SERVES 4

Another fun spin on a classic, these stuffed peppers are a lot like tacos, just without a shell! While the filling is prepared, the peppers are cooking at the same time in the oven, then you load up the peppers with the filling and top them with cheese. You'll be enjoying a simple and satisfying meal in no time.

INGREDIENTS

- 3 bell peppers, halved lengthwise
- 3 tablespoons canola oil, divided
- ½ pound ground beef
- 1 medium onion, diced
- 1 tablespoon chili powder
- ¼ teaspoon garlic powder
- ¼ teaspoon dried oregano
- ½ teaspoon paprika
- 1½ teaspoon cumin
- 1 teaspoon salt
- 1 teaspoon pepper
- 1 cup black beans, drained and rinsed
- 1 cup frozen corn
- 1 cup shredded Mexican blend cheese

DIRECTIONS

1 Preheat the oven to 375°F. Place pepper halves on a baking dish, drizzle with 2 tablespoons of oil, and bake for 20 minutes.

2 Meanwhile, in a large pan over medium heat, warm the remaining oil. Add the onions and cook about 4-5 minutes, until they are translucent. Add the beef and cook about 5 minutes, until no longer pink. Stir in the chili powder, garlic powder, oregano, paprika, cumin, salt, pepper, beans, and corn to the meat and onions, cooking for 5 minutes, stirring occasionally.

3 Remove peppers from the oven and let them cool slightly, draining off any excess water and oil. Set the oven to broil on high, spoon-fill each pepper with the meat mixture, top with cheese, and broil for about 2 minutes, until the cheese is melted.

RECIPES

Asparagus and Ricotta Frittata	**139**
Broccoli Mushroom Quiche	**141**
Falafel Pitas	**143**
Gnocchi with Palomino Sauce	**145**
Roasted Tandoori Cauliflower	**147**
Spring Pizza	**149**
Tomato, Avocado, and Cucumber Salad	**151**
Vegetarian Taco Salad	**153**

Whether you have a vegetarian friend coming over for dinner and you don't know what to make, or you're just looking to add more vegetables into your diet, this chapter is filled with satisfying and delicious meals. From the egg-filled favorites like Frittatas and Quiches to the more worldly flavors like Falafel Pitas, Roasted Tandoori Cauliflower, and Vegetarian Taco Salad, these dishes will impress the vegetarian in your life. And they may make the idea of adding more veggies to your plate much more exciting. This chapter may just flip the way you think about eating vegetarian meals!

VEGETARIAN

ROASTED TANDOORI CAULIFLOWER PAGE 147

VEGETARIAN

ASPARAGUS AND RICOTTA FRITTATA

SERVES 4

Essentially a quiche without the crust or a fancy baked omelet. We've taken some of our favorite springtime vegetables and paired them with creamy ricotta cheese, making this a dish that's a truly show-stopping meal. If you've never had a frittata, you'll enjoy the delicate flavors and will likely start looking up more recipes for them! (Psst! Check our website!)

INGREDIENTS

- 8 eggs
- ½ cup whole milk, divided
- 1 teaspoon salt
- ½ teaspoon pepper
- 1 cup ricotta cheese
- 1 tablespoon canola oil
- 1 leek, chopped
- 10 asparagus spears, cut diagonally
- 1 tablespoon butter

DIRECTIONS

1 Preheat the oven to 350°F. In a medium bowl, beat together the eggs, ¼ cup of milk, salt, and pepper. In a small bowl, stir together the remaining ¼ cup of milk and ricotta cheese.

2 In a large oven-safe skillet over medium heat, warm the oil. Add the leeks and asparagus, cook for about 4 minutes, until the leeks begin to soften. Transfer to a plate.

3 In the same skillet, melt the butter, pour in the egg mixture and cook about 2 minutes, until eggs begin to set. Swirl the ricotta cheese mixture over the eggs and add the vegetables on top. Bake about 10-15 minutes, until fully set. Set oven to broil on high for 5 minutes or until the frittata becomes golden brown on top.

VEGETARIAN

BROCCOLI MUSHROOM QUICHE

SERVES 4

A savory dish fit for breakfast, lunch, or dinner it's fit for any meal! With crisp broccoli, caramelized onions, tender mushrooms, and shredded cheese, there's really no reason not to love this quiche!

INGREDIENTS

- 1 frozen pie crust, thawed
- 2 tablespoons canola oil
- 1 small onion, chopped
- 1 cup broccoli florets, halved
- ½ cup sliced mushrooms
- 8 eggs
- ½ cup shredded cheddar cheese
- 1 teaspoon salt
- ½ teaspoon pepper

DIRECTIONS

1 Preheat the oven to 350°F. Place the pie crust into a pie pan, poke the bottom of the crust with a fork, and pre-bake for 15 minutes until lightly browned.

2 In a pan over medium heat, warm the oil. Add the onion, cooking about 5-7 minutes, until they have softened. Add the broccoli and mushrooms, cooking an additional 5-7 minutes, until the mushrooms have shrunk and start to darken in color.

3 In a medium bowl, beat the eggs. Add the cooked vegetables to the pie crust, sprinkle with cheese, and pour in the egg mixture. Cook for 45 minutes or until lightly browned. Let cool for 5 minutes before serving.

VEGETARIAN

FALAFEL PITAS

SERVES 4

Falafel is one of those popular Middle Eastern dishes that can seem a bit tricky to tackle. This recipe is stripped down to its simplest form, making them not only easy but downright fun to make! Load up a few in a pita with veggies and drizzled with some yogurt sauce and you have a meal that will please vegetarians and meat-eaters alike!

SALAD

- ½ cup cherry tomatoes, halved
- 1 small cucumber, diced
- ½ small red onion, diced
- 1 tablespoon canola oil
- ½ teaspoon salt
- Pepper, to taste

YOGURT SAUCE

- 1 cup Greek yogurt
- 1 tablespoon lemon juice
- 1 tablespoon freshly chopped dill
- ½ teaspoon salt
- Pepper, to taste

FALAFEL

- 1 (15-ounce) can chickpeas, drained
- ½ small red onion, chopped
- 3 garlic cloves, minced
- 3 tablespoons flour
- 2 tablespoons freshly chopped parsley
- 1 teaspoon cumin
- 1 teaspoon ground coriander
- ⅛ teaspoon ground cardamom
- 1 teaspoon salt
- ¼ teaspoon pepper
- Canola oil, for frying
- Pita pockets

DIRECTIONS

1 In a small bowl, toss together the tomatoes, cucumber, onion, oil, salt, and pepper. Set aside. In a separate small bowl, stir together the yogurt, lemon juice, oil, dill, salt, and pepper. Cover and set aside.

2 In a food processor fitted with an 'S' blade, add the chickpeas, onion, garlic, flour, parsley, cumin, coriander, cardamom, salt, and pepper. Pulse until a coarse meal forms, being careful not to let the mixture become a paste. (This can be made ahead and refrigerated for up to 2 days.)

3 In a large skillet or Dutch oven, heat 1-inch of oil over medium heat. Meanwhile, using your hands, form the falafel mixture into round balls, using about 2 tablespoons of the mixture per ball.

4 Gently place the balls into the oil, cooking about 2-3 minutes per side, until browned, cooking about 5 or 6 at a time. When done, place on a paper towel-lined plate to cool for about 2 minutes. Serve in a pita, layered with the yogurt sauce, and topped with the salad.

Quick and Easy Meals

VEGETARIAN

GNOCCHI WITH PALOMINO SAUCE

SERVES 4

By far one of the most popular recipes featured on our website. Palomino sauce is kind of like the perfect combination of marinara and an alfredo sauce. Served here simply with gnocchi, it would also work amazingly in lasagna or served over pasta.

INGREDIENTS

- 1 (16-ounce) package gnocchi
- 1 tablespoon butter
- 2 garlic cloves, minced
- 1 small onion, thinly sliced
- 1 tablespoon flour
- ¾ cup milk
- 1 cup heavy whipping cream
- ½ teaspoon salt
- 1½ cups marinara sauce
- ¼ cup parmesan cheese, freshly grated

DIRECTIONS

1 In a large pot, bring water to a boil, add the gnocchi and cook according to package directions.

2 In a pan over medium heat, melt the butter. Add the garlic and onion, cooking about 5-7 minutes, until onions are translucent. Whisk in the flour, cooking for 1 minute. Slowly stir in the milk, cream, and salt, continuing to stir until it begins to simmer. Stir in the marinara sauce, cooking for an additional 10-15 minutes, stirring occasionally. Serve over the gnocchi and sprinkle with parmesan.

VEGETARIAN
ROASTED TANDOORI CAULIFLOWER

SERVES 4

These Indian-spiced nuggets of yum will have everyone raving! Their unique flavor with freshly squeezed lemon juice will have even the pickiest of eaters asking for more! Serve it with a side dish or salad for a satisfying meal!

INGREDIENTS

- ½ cup almond butter
- 4 teaspoons tandoori paste
- 2 teaspoons water
- 1 head cauliflower, cut into 1-inch florets
- 2 tablespoons canola oil
- ½ lemon

DIRECTIONS

1 Preheat the oven to 450°F. In a large bowl, stir together the almond butter, tandoori paste, and water. Add the cauliflower and toss to coat.

2 Oil a roasting pan and spread the cauliflower in an even layer. Cook for 10-15 minutes until the cauliflower is tender. Turn the oven to broil on high and cook for 2-3 minutes, until the tops begin to brown.

3 Squeeze the lemon over the cauliflower before serving.

VEGETARIAN

SPRING PIZZA

SERVES 4

If the idea of a pizza without a sauce has you cursing us under your breath, just trust us! Even some of us in the test kitchens were skeptical until we tried it. This pizza is loaded with fresh flavors that you likely won't even notice the lack of sauce! If you can't bear it, feel free to add some, we promise we won't tell.

INGREDIENTS

- 1 tablespoon canola oil
- 1 pound frozen pizza dough, thawed
- 1 cup thinly sliced leek
- 2 cups shredded mozzarella cheese
- 6 asparagus spears, cut into 1-inch pieces
- 1½ cups chopped escarole
- ½ cup sliced cherry tomatoes

DIRECTIONS

1 Preheat the oven to 500°F. On a greased baking sheet, shape the pizza dough into an approximate 11x16-inch rectangle.

2 Top the dough with the leeks, cheese, and asparagus. Bake for about 8 minutes. Carefully remove from the oven and sprinkle the escarole and tomatoes over the top. Return to the oven and bake for about 5-8 minutes, until the cheese has browned and the escarole is wilted. Let sit for about 5 minutes before serving.

VEGETARIAN

TOMATO, AVOCADO, AND CUCUMBER SALAD

SERVES 4

Simple recipes become extraordinary when you choose fresh, in-season produce that really takes a recipe like this to the next level! This hearty but simple salad makes a great side dish or lunch. The fresh vegetables pair perfectly with the tangy dressing and smooth feta. You'll be hooked!

INGREDIENTS

- 1½ cups halved cherry tomatoes
- 1 cucumber, diced
- 1 avocado, diced
- 4 ounces feta cheese, crumbled
- 4 green onions, sliced diagonally
- 2 tablespoons minced parsley
- 2 tablespoons canola oil
- 1 tablespoon red wine vinegar
- 1 teaspoon salt
- ½ teaspoon pepper

DIRECTIONS

1 In a large bowl, combine the tomatoes, cucumber, avocado, feta, green onions, and parsley.

2 In a small bowl, stir together the oil, vinegar, salt, and pepper.

3 Pour the dressing over the salad and gently toss to combine.

VEGETARIAN

VEGETARIAN TACO SALAD

SERVES 4

Everything you love about a taco piled onto a bed of fresh greens. Getting rid of the meat in this vegetarian twist on a taco doesn't disappoint as it throws a couple of head-turning twists at you that not only make it healthier but also make it just a downright fun way to eat it!

SPANISH RICE

- 2 tablespoons canola oil
- 1 small onion, diced
- 2 garlic cloves, minced
- 1 teaspoon cumin
- 1 teaspoon chili powder
- ¼ teaspoon pepper
- ¼ teaspoon paprika
- 1 (10-ounce) can Mexican stewed tomatoes
- 1 (14.5-ounce) can chicken broth
- ½ cup tomato sauce
- 1 cup uncooked rice

INGREDIENTS

- 2 medium avocados, diced
- 1 lime, juiced
- Salt, to taste
- 2 cups salsa
- 1 cup sour cream
- ½ cup finely chopped cilantro
- 3 heads romaine lettuce, chopped
- ½ head iceberg lettuce, chopped
- 1 (15-ounce) can pinto beans, drained
- 1 (15-ounce) can black beans, drained
- Prepared Spanish rice
- 4 ounces shredded colby jack cheese
- Tortilla chips, for garnish

DIRECTIONS

1 In a medium saucepan over medium heat, warm the oil. Add the onions and garlic, cooking about 5-7 minutes, until translucent.

2 Stir in the cumin, chili powder, pepper, paprika, tomatoes, chicken broth, tomato sauce, and rice. Bring to a boil, then reduce the heat to low, cover, and cook for about 20 minutes, until the rice is tender and the liquids are fully absorbed. (If liquids are absorbed while the rice is still firm, add ¼-½ cup more water and continue to cook until the rice is tender.)

3 In a small bowl, stir together the avocados, lime juice, and salt. In a separate small bowl, stir together the salsa, sour cream, and cilantro. Set both aside.

4 In a large serving bowl, layer the romaine, iceberg, beans, and rice. Top with the avocado mixture, cheese, tortilla chips, and the salsa dressing.

Quick and Easy Meals

RECIPES

Beef Barley Soup	**157**
Black Bean Soup	**159**
Chicken & Dumplings	**161**
Egg Drop Soup	**163**
Lightened Cheese Soup	**165**
Loaded Potato Soup	**167**
Minestrone Soup	**169**
Sausage and Bean Soup	**171**
Stuffed Cabbage Soup	**173**
Tomato, Basil, & Gnocchi Soup	**175**

Soups are great for those chilly nights when you need something hearty and delicious to warm you up — but in our test kitchen, we love soup all year round! This chapter is packed full of soup recipes that will wow your taste buds, from classic comforts like Chicken & Dumplings and Loaded Potato to more adventurous ones like Tomato, Basil, & Gnocchi and Egg Drop. With such a wide variety of flavor combinations, you'll have the perfect soup recipe for any occasion, any time of the year.

SOUPS

TOMATO, BASIL, & GNOCCHI SOUP PAGE 175

BEEF BARLEY SOUP

SERVES 6

A classic favorite for many generations. Our version comes together quickly, as quickly as a soup of this fashion can be made, while still giving you the tender bits of beef and rich, savory broth you look for in a hearty soup like this one.

INGREDIENTS

- 2 tablespoons canola oil, divided
- 2 pounds stew meat, cubed
- 1 medium onion, diced
- 3 carrots, diced
- 2 celery stalks, sliced
- 8 ounces baby bella mushrooms, sliced
- 2 (32-ounce) containers beef broth
- 2 cups water
- 1 teaspoon onion powder
- 1 bay leaf
- ½ teaspoon dried thyme
- 1 tablespoon chopped parsley
- 1 teaspoon poultry seasoning, such as Old Bay®
- 2 beef bullion cubes
- 1 cup pearl barley
- 1½ teaspoons salt
- ½ teaspoon pepper
- 1 French baguette, for serving

DIRECTIONS

1 In a large pot over medium-high heat, warm 1 tablespoon of the oil. Add in the stew meat and cook for 10 minutes, or until evenly browned. Transfer to a plate and set aside.

2 Reduce the heat to medium, add the remaining tablespoon of oil and the onions. Cook about 10 minutes, stirring occasionally until the onions have softened. Add in the carrots, celery, and mushrooms and cook for 5 minutes. Return the meat to the pot, stir in the broth, water, onion powder, bay leaf, thyme, parsley, poultry seasoning, bullion cubes, barley, salt, and pepper. Bring the soup to a simmer, partially cover, and cook for 40 minutes, or until the meat is tender and the barley is fully cooked.

3 Serve with a slice of baguette.

SOUPS

BLACK BEAN SOUP

SERVES 6

This isn't your average black bean soup! We've dressed up our version with a southwest flavor profile that's both filling and fresh. Serve topped with cilantro, tomatoes, and a squeeze of lime, or with salsa and a poached egg (that's how our boss likes it). No matter which way you choose to garnish it, we know it's going to become an instant hit!

INGREDIENTS

- 1 tablespoon canola oil
- 1 small onion, chopped
- 6 garlic cloves, minced
- 2 teaspoons cumin
- 1 teaspoon salt
- ½ teaspoon pepper
- 1 teaspoon chili powder
- 1 teaspoon dried oregano
- ⅛ teaspoon cayenne pepper
- 1 (14.5-ounce) can chicken broth
- 4 (15-ounce) cans black beans, drained
- 1 (14.5-ounce) can diced tomatoes
- 1 cup cooked rice

TOPPINGS

- Grape tomatoes
- Cilantro
- Tortilla strips
- Grated cheese
- Lime wedges

DIRECTIONS

1 In a large pot over medium-high heat, warm the oil. Add the onions and garlic, cook for about 10 minutes, or until translucent. Stir in the cumin, salt, pepper, chili powder, oregano, cayenne, chicken broth, black beans, and tomatoes. Simmer for 25-30 minutes.

2 Add the rice and simmer for 5 minutes. Serve with choice of toppings.

Note: For a creamier consistency, puree the soup mixture in a high-speed blender or food processor, working in batches. Pour each batch back into the pot and stir together.

SOUPS

EGG DROP SOUP

SERVES 6

Egg drop is a fan-favorite among Chinese takeout restaurants and is most easily recognized by its vibrant yellow color. The brightness of the broth is usually an indication that food coloring has been added. Since food coloring doesn't actually enhance the flavor, we've swapped it out for nutrient-rich snow peas and bean sprouts to make this a nutritious, well-rounded meal that tastes amazing!

INGREDIENTS

- 1 (32-ounce) container chicken broth
- 3 cups water
- 4 teaspoons low-sodium soy sauce
- 2 teaspoons fresh grated ginger
- ¼ teaspoon pepper
- 8 ounces fresh snow peas, cut into bite-sized pieces
- 1 cup fresh bean sprouts
- 1 tablespoon rice vinegar
- 1 teaspoon toasted sesame oil
- 1 teaspoon salt
- 2 eggs, beaten
- 4 green onions, sliced

DIRECTIONS

1 In a large pot over high heat, add the chicken broth, water, soy sauce, ginger, pepper, snow peas, and bean sprouts. Bring to a boil, reduce the heat to medium to maintain a simmer. Stir in the rice vinegar, sesame oil, and salt, cooking for 5 minutes, or until the vegetables are tender.

2 Gently pour in the eggs while stirring. Continue stirring for two minutes or until the eggs are thoroughly cooked. Stir in the green onions and serve.

LIGHTENED CHEESE SOUP

SERVES 4

Cream-based cheese soups are delicious but not always the best for you. We've tweaked our approach with this one by making the base with chicken broth and flour. The result is the same thick and creamy texture of a traditional cheese soup without the additional calories. Feel free to add in broccoli — broccoli cheddar soup, anyone? — mushrooms, or even rice!

INGREDIENTS

- 4 tablespoons butter
- 1 celery stalk, minced
- 1 carrot, minced
- 1 small onion, diced
- 2 garlic cloves, minced
- 6 tablespoons flour
- 1 (14.5-ounce) can chicken broth
- 2½ cups water
- 2 cups shredded mild cheddar
- 1 cup shredded sharp cheddar
- 3 drops aromatic bitters

DIRECTIONS

1 In a large pot over medium-high heat, melt the butter. Add the celery, carrots, onions, and garlic and cook for about 5 minutes, or until the onions are translucent. Stir in the flour and cook for 1-2 minutes. Slowly add in the chicken broth a ½ cup at a time and stir until smooth. Pour in the water and bring the mixture to a simmer cooking for 20 minutes.

2 Stir in the cheese one cup at a time, waiting for the cheese to melt before adding more. Stir in the bitters and serve immediately.

LOADED POTATO SOUP

SERVES 6

This soup is everything you love on a loaded baked potato, all mixed into a big pot! Finished off with bacon, cheese, and fresh green onions, this creamy and flavor-packed soup will be loved by everyone!

INGREDIENTS

- 6 cups chicken broth
- 3 pounds russet potatoes, peeled and quartered
- 6 tablespoons butter
- 1 large onion, diced
- 1 garlic clove, minced
- 3 tablespoons flour
- ½ cup whole milk or heavy cream
- 4 ounces cream cheese
- 2 cups shredded medium cheddar cheese
- 1 teaspoon salt
- 1 teaspoon pepper
- 1 green onion, sliced
- 3 ounces shredded mild cheddar cheese
- 12 slices thick-cut bacon, cooked and crumbled
- ½ cup sour cream

DIRECTIONS

1 In a large pot over medium heat, add the chicken broth and potatoes. Cover and cook for 20 minutes, or until the potatoes are tender.

2 Meanwhile, in a large pan over medium heat, melt the butter. Add the onions and cook 7-10 minutes, until the onions are translucent. Stir in the garlic and flour, cook for 1-2 minutes, then slowly whisk in the milk.

3 Once the potatoes are tender, pour the onion mixture into the pot. Gently mash the potatoes and cook for 10 minutes, or until the mixture thickens. Add in the cream cheese, cheddar, salt, and pepper, and stir until the cheese melts.

4 Serve topped with bacon, cheese, sour cream, and green onion.

SOUPS

MINESTRONE SOUP

SERVES 6

Believe it or not, Minestrone soup has no set recipe! This Italian favorite was created by using up whatever you had on hand, and could be made with meat or entirely vegetarian. Minestrone's most common ingredients include beans, onions, celery, carrots, broth, tomatoes, and a starch, like rice or pasta. This is our favorite way to serve this traditional Italian dish, but don't be afraid to change it up and make it fun for everyone!

INGREDIENTS

- 4 tablespoons butter
- 1 medium onion, chopped
- 2 carrots, peeled and chopped
- 2 celery stalks, chopped
- 2 cups chopped summer vegetables, such as zucchini and yellow squash
- 3 (14.5-ounce) cans chicken broth
- 3 (14.5-ounce) cans beef broth
- 1 cup water
- 1 (28-ounce) can diced tomatoes
- 1 (15-ounce) can white kidney beans, drained
- ¼ cup tomato paste
- 4 garlic cloves, minced
- 2 teaspoons dried parsley
- 1 teaspoon salt
- ½ cup chopped fresh basil
- ¼ teaspoon pepper
- 1 cup uncooked short pasta, such as ditalini
- ⅓ cup parmesan cheese
- 1 (15-ounce) can chickpeas
- 1 cup half & half
- 2 cups baby spinach

DIRECTIONS

1 In a large pot over medium-high heat, melt the butter. Add in the onions, carrots, celery, and summer vegetables and cook for 5-7 minutes, or until the onions are translucent. Reduce heat to medium and add in the chicken broth, beef broth, water, diced tomatoes, kidney beans, tomato paste, garlic, parsley, salt, basil, and pepper. Cook for 20 minutes, partially covered.

2 Stir in the noodles, parmesan, and chickpeas, and cook for 20 minutes, or until the noodles are completely cooked through. Stir in the half & half and spinach until just wilted, then serve.

Quick and Easy Meals

SAUSAGE AND BEAN SOUP

SERVES 6

This soup is big on flavor and is so simple to make! We know you'll keep coming back to this recipe again and again! Italian sausage and cream add heartiness while the kale and navy beans add nutrients. Serve with a slice of fresh-baked French bread, and you'll be in quick-dinner heaven!

INGREDIENTS

- 1 tablespoon canola oil
- 1 pound ground Italian sausage
- 2 garlic cloves, minced
- ½ teaspoon onion powder
- 1 (32-ounce) container chicken broth
- 1 cup water
- 1 bunch kale, stems removed and finely chopped or shredded
- 4 (15-ounce) cans navy beans, drained
- ½ cup half & half
- 1 teaspoon salt
- ½ teaspoon pepper
- 1 loaf French bread, sliced

DIRECTIONS

1 In a large pot over medium heat, warm the oil. Add the sausage and cook about 8 minutes, until browned. Remove the sausage and set aside.

2 Add the garlic and onion powder to the pot and cook about 1 minute, until fragrant. Pour in the chicken broth and water, then add in the kale. Bring the mixture to a boil, then reduce the heat to a simmer and cook for 5 minutes. Add in the beans and sausage and cook for 20 minutes.

3 Stir in the half & half, salt, and pepper until just combined. Serve with sliced French bread.

STUFFED CABBAGE SOUP

SERVES 6

Stuffed cabbage is comfort food to many but can be a bit time consuming to make. We've simplified this popular dish by combining the same ingredients into a soup. You'll love it as much as the classic — maybe even more because it's so easy!

INGREDIENTS

- 1 teaspoon canola oil
- 1 medium onion, diced
- 2 garlic cloves, minced
- 1 pound ground beef
- 2 red bell peppers, chopped
- 1 small cabbage, chopped or torn into small pieces
- 1 teaspoon salt
- ½ teaspoon pepper
- 1 teaspoon paprika
- ¼ teaspoon crushed red pepper flakes
- 1 tablespoon Worcestershire sauce
- 1 bay leaf
- 1 cup uncooked brown rice
- 1 (32-ounce) container beef broth
- 3 cups water
- 2½ cups tomato juice

DIRECTIONS

1 In a large pot over medium heat, warm the oil. Add the onions and garlic and cook for about 5-7 minutes, or until the onions are translucent. Add the ground beef and cook for 5-8 minutes, until no longer pink. Stir in the bell peppers, cabbage, salt, pepper, paprika, pepper flakes, Worcestershire sauce, bay leaf, brown rice, beef broth, water, and tomato juice. Bring the mixture to a boil, then reduce the heat to a simmer. Cook for 25 minutes, or until the cabbage is tender.

TOMATO, BASIL, & GNOCCHI SOUP

SERVES 6

This soup has become a go-to for many of us here at the test kitchen because it really can't be any easier to make! Full of fresh flavors, simple ingredients, and good quality gnocchi (you could even make your own if you want!), we know this is going to become a fast favorite!

INGREDIENTS

- 2 (28-ounce) cans stewed tomatoes
- 1 (14.5-ounce) can chicken broth
- 2 teaspoons dried oregano
- 1 teaspoon salt
- 1 (16-ounce) package gnocchi
- 2 tablespoons fresh basil, chopped
- 1 crusty Italian bread loaf, optional for serving

DIRECTIONS

1 Using kitchen shears or a knife, coarsely chop one can of tomatoes. Add the second can of tomatoes to a blender or food processor and puree until smooth.

2 In a large pot over medium-high heat, stir in tomatoes, broth, oregano, and salt. Bring the mixture to a boil and cook for 3 minutes, stirring often. Reduce the heat to a simmer and cook for 5 minutes.

3 Return the heat to medium-high and add the gnocchi. Cook for 3-4 minutes, then remove the pot from the heat and stir in the basil. Serve with a slice of crusty Italian bread.

STILL HUNGRY?

Well, there's plenty more where that came from!
For more recipes, books, and videos, visit

BESTRECIPES.CO

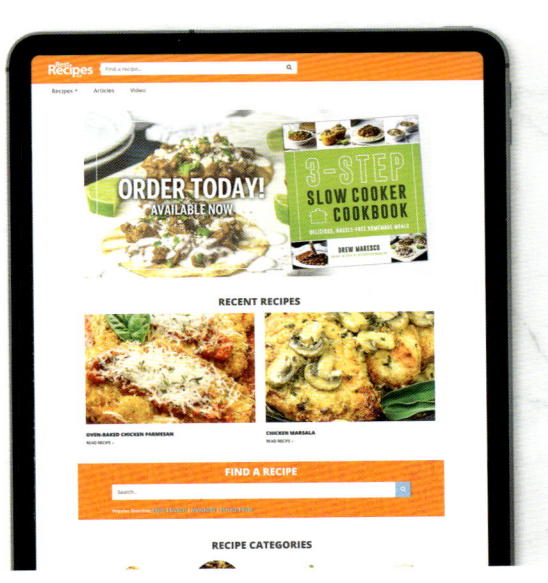

ABOUT BEST RECIPES

Best Recipes Media Group develops both print and digital resources to help busy people get back into the kitchen and make their own meals with recipes that are quick and easy for everyone, regardless of cooking skill.

ACKNOWLEDGMENTS

This book represents the talent and creativity of many individuals. Some of their works originally appearing in our magazine are now featured here. Thank you to Dallyn Maresco, Melanie Stansbury, Cheryl Maresco, Paula Collins, Regina Roberts, Nicole Hanson, Ashley Holman, Susan Williams, Deanne Boucher, Jan Hanson, Pamela Hackett, and Demetrius Means for their contributions to our publications and this cookbook.

Photography throughout this book is made possible by Drew Maresco, Dallyn Maresco, Cheryl Maresco, and James Stefiuk. Thank you for the stunning images that represent these recipes.

A special thanks to the editors Catherine Morin and Dallyn Maresco for their diligence and expertise in making this book possible.

We would also like to thank Ashley Horst, Gina Weinzierl, Sara Christian, and Katie Decker for all their involvement in making Best Recipes Media Group possible.

ABOUT THE AUTHORS

DREW MARESCO

Author and self-taught cook with a mind for creating unique, simple, and delicious recipes. Inspired at a young age while sitting on grandma's countertop, he assisted with everything she baked. After starting what began as a small food blog, to what is now the website and various print publications of BestRecipes.co, he strives to make dinner simple and easy for everyone.

DALLYN MARESCO

Starting as a writer, then editor and food stylist, she loves the art behind everything that she does. She learned how to cook at a young age while baking with grandma, which quickly became one of her favorite things. Initially, her writing background is what brought her to the food team at Best Recipes, but she quickly became an integral part of the operations, and now her work is seen in every recipe we publish.

INDEX

A

Almond
　In Thai Shrimp Salad 97
　Butter
　　　In Roasted Tandoori Cauliflower 147
Aloha Bbq Burger Sliders 35
Anchovy
　In Shredded Chicken Caesar Salad 81
Angel Hair Pasta
　In Shrimp Scampi with Angel Hair 115
Apple Cider Vinegar
　In Chopped Kale Salad 87
Aromatic Bitters
　In Lightened Cheese Soup 165
Asian 10
Asian Seared Salmon with Baby Bok Choy 13
Asparagus
　In Dijon Salmon 111
　In Spring Pizza 149
Asparagus and Ricotta Frittata 139
Asparagus Spears
　In Asparagus and Ricotta Frittata 139
Avocado
　In Classic Cobb Salad with Creamy Garlic Dressing 83
　In Fiesta Chicken Burger 43
　In Tomato, Avocado, and Cucumber Salad 151
　In Vegetarian Taco Salad 153

B

Baby Arugula
　In Poached Salmon & Pecan Salad 93
Baby Bok Choy
　In Asian Seared Salmon with Baby Bok Choy 13
　In Teriyaki Chicken 19
Bacon
　In Carbonara 57
　In Chicken Quesadillas 123
　In Classic Cobb Salad with Creamy Garlic Dressing 83
　In Loaded Potato Soup 167
　In Mac and Cheese 63
　In Shrimp with Bacon & Cheesy Grits 117
　In Tortellini Alfredo with Bacon 77
Balsamic Vinegar
　In Tomato Beet Salad 99
Banh Mi with Sriracha Mayo 15
Bao Buns
　In Sticky Pork Sliders 21
Basil
　In Meatball Marinara Submarine Sandwiches 47
　In Mediterranean Meatballs 49
　In Minestrone Soup 169
　In Spaghetti and Meatballs 69
　In Tomato, Basil, & Gnocchi Soup 175
　In Tomato Beet Salad 99
　Leaves Of
　　　In Chopped Kale Salad 87
Basmati Rice
　In Asian Seared Salmon with Baby Bok Choy 13
　In Beef and Broccoli 17
　In Pineapple Fried Rice 27
　In Quick Pepper Steak 29
　In Sweet and Sour Chicken 25
　In Teriyaki Chicken 19
　In Thai Green Curry 31
Bay Leaf
　In Beef Barley Soup 157
　In Chicken & Dumplings 161
　In Stuffed Cabbage Soup 173
BBQ Sauce
　In Aloha BBQ Burger Sliders 35
Bean Sprout
　In Egg Drop Soup 163

Beef
　Broth
　　　　In Beef Barley Soup 157
　　　　In Quick Pepper Steak 29
　　　　In Stuffed Cabbage Soup 173
　Ground
　　　　In Aloha BBQ Burger Sliders 35
　　　　In Classic Beef Tacos 121
　　　　In Meatball Marinara Submarine Sandwiches 47
　　　　In Meaty Mozzarella Pasta Bake 67
　　　　In Mediterranean Meatballs 49
　　　　In Spaghetti and Meatballs 69
　　　　In Stroganoff Meatballs 71
　　　　In Tex-Mex Skillet 133
　　　　In Tex Mex Stuffed Peppers 135
　Low-Sodium
　　　　In Stroganoff Meatballs 71
Beef and Broccoli 17
Beef Barley Soup 157
Beef Bullion Cubes
　In Beef Barley Soup 157
Black Beans
　In Black Bean Quinoa Burger 37
　In Black Beans Soup 159
　In Chicken Quesadillas 123
　In Tex-Mex Skillet 133
　In Tex Mex Stuffed Peppers 135
　In Vegetarian Taco Salad 153
Black Beans Soup 159
Black Bean Quinoa Burger 37
Black Peppercorns
　In Poached Salmon & Pecan Salad 93
Breadcrumbs
　In Fiesta Chicken Burger 43
　In Meatball Marinara Submarine Sandwiches 47
　In Mediterranean Meatballs 49
　In Spaghetti and Meatballs 69
　In Spaghetti with Chicken Parmesan Meatballs 59
　In Stroganoff Meatballs 71
Brioche Buns
　In Fiesta Chicken Burger 43
Broccoli
　In Beef and Broccoli 17
　Florets
　　　　In Broccoli Mushroom Quiche 141
Broccoli Mushroom Quiche 141
Brown Rice
　In Stuffed Cabbage Soup 173
Burgers & Sandwiches 32
Butter
　In Asparagus and Ricotta Frittata 139
　In Chicken & Dumplings 161
　In Creole Shrimp Pasta 103
　In Gnocchi with Palomino Sauce 145
　In Lemon and Herb Butter Salmon 109
　In Lightened Cheese Soup 165
　In Loaded Potato Soup 167
　In Mac and Cheese 63
　In Minestrone Soup 169
　In Shrimp Scampi with Angel Hair 115
　In Shrimp with Bacon & Cheesy Grits 117
　In Tortellini Alfredo with Bacon 77
Buttermilk
　In Shrimp with Bacon & Cheesy Grits 117

C

Cabbage
　In Stuffed Cabbage Soup 173
Cajun Seasoning
　In Cajun Shrimp Po' Boy 39
Cajun Shrimp Po' Boy 39
Canola Oil
　In Aloha BBQ Burger Sliders 35

INDEX

In Asian Seared Salmon with Baby Bok Choy 13
In Asparagus and Ricotta Frittata 139
In Banh Mi with Sriracha Mayo 15
In Beef Barley Soup 157
In Beef and Broccoli 17
In Black Bean Quinoa Burger 37
In Black Beans Soup 159
In Broccoli Mushroom Quiche 141
In Steak Fajitas 125
In Chicken Quesadillas 123
In Classic Beef Tacos 121
In Creole Shrimp Pasta 103
In Dijon Salmon 111
In Fiesta Chicken Burger 43
In Garlic and Parmesan Salmon 107
In Penne with Lemon Cream Sauce and Spinach 61
In Philly Cheesesteak 51
In Pimento Cheeseburgers 53
In Pineapple Fried Rice 27
In Quick Pepper Steak 29
In Roasted Tandoori Cauliflower 147
In Sausage and Bean Soup 171
In Sausage, Sweet Potato, and Kale Pasta 75
In Seasoned Whitefish with Sun-Dried Tomatoes & Spinach 113
In Shrimp Scampi with Angel Hair 115
In Spaghetti and Meatballs 69
In Spicy Chicken Lo Mein 23
In Spring Pizza 149
In Steak Fajita Salad 95
In Sticky Pork Sliders 21
In Stroganoff Meatballs 71
In Stuffed Cabbage Soup 173
In Stuffed Poblano Peppers 131
In Sweet and Sour Chicken 25
In Teriyaki Chicken 19
In Tex-Mex Skillet 133

In Tex Mex Stuffed Peppers 135
In Thai Green Curry 31
In Tomato, Avocado, and Cucumber Salad 151
In Tortellini Alfredo with Bacon 77
Carbonara 57
Cardamom
  In Falafel Pitas 143
Carrot
  In Banh Mi with Sriracha Mayo 15
  In Beef Barley Soup 157
  In Black Bean Quinoa Burger 37
  In Chicken & Dumplings 161
  In Lightened Cheese Soup 165
  In Minestrone Soup 169
  In Pineapple Fried Rice 27
  In Spicy Chicken Lo Mein 23
  In Thai Shrimp Salad 97
Cauliflower
  In Roasted Tandoori Cauliflower 147
Cavatappi Pasta
  In Meaty Mozzarella Pasta Bake 67
Celery
  In Beef Barley Soup 157
  Stalks
    In Chicken & Dumplings 161
    In Lightened Cheese Soup 165
    In Minestrone Soup 169
    In Spicy Chicken Lo Mein 23
    In Sticky Pork Sliders 21t
Cheese
  Cheddar
    In Broccoli Mushroom Quiche 141
    In Lightened Cheese Soup 165
    In Loaded Potato Soup 167
    In Mac and Cheese 63
    In Pimento Cheeseburgers 53
    In Shrimp with Bacon & Cheesy Grits 117

In Steak Fajitas 125
In Steak Fajita Salad 95
In Stuffed Poblano Peppers 131
In Tex-Mex Skillet 133

Cream
In Loaded Potato Soup 167

Colby Jack
In Chicken Quesadillas 123
In Classic Cobb Salad with Creamy Garlic Dressing 83
In Green Chili Chicken Enchilada Casserole 127
In Vegetarian Taco Salad 153

Cream
In Green Chili Chicken Enchilada Casserole 127
In Orecchiette with Tomato Cream Sauce 65

Feta
In Greek Salad 85
In Tomato, Avocado, and Cucumber Salad 151
In Tomato Beet Salad 99

In Stuffed Poblano Peppers 131

Mexican Blend
In Tex Mex Stuffed Peppers 135

Mozzarella
In Chicken Parm Sandwich 41
In Meatball Marinara Submarine Sandwiches 47
In Spinach & Ricotta Stuffed Shells 73
In Spring Pizza 149

Parmesan
In Chicken Parm Sandwich 41
In Creole Shrimp Pasta 103
In Garlic and Parmesan Salmon 107
In Gnocchi with Palomino Sauce 145
In Mac and Cheese 63
In Meatball Marinara Submarine Sandwiches 47

In Minestrone Soup 169
In Orecchiette with Tomato Cream Sauce 65
In Shredded Chicken Caesar Salad 81
In Spaghetti and Meatballs 69

Pepper Jack
In Fiesta Chicken Burger 43

Provolone
In Philly Cheesesteak 51

Ricotta
In Asparagus and Ricotta Frittata 139

Swiss
In Maurice Salad 89

Tortellini
In Tortellini Alfredo with Bacon 77

Chorizo
In Stuffed Poblano Peppers 131

Chia Seeds
In Raspberry Quinoa Salad 91

Chicken
Breast
In Chicken Parm Sandwich 41
In Chicken Quesadillas 123
In Classic Cobb Salad with Creamy Garlic Dressing 83
In Lemon Chicken Pita Wraps with Tzatziki 45
In Shredded Chicken Caesar Salad 81
In Teriyaki Chicken 19

Broth
In Sweet and Sour Chicken 25
In Thai Green Curry 31
In Black Beans Soup 159
In Chicken & Dumplings 161
In Egg Drop Soup 163
In Lightened Cheese Soup 165
In Loaded Potato Soup 167
In Minestrone Soup 169

Quick and Easy Meals **183**

INDEX

    In Sausage and Bean Soup 171
    In Sticky Pork Sliders 21
    In Tomato, Basil, & Gnocchi Soup 175
  In Chicken & Dumplings 161
  In Fiesta Chicken Burger 43
  In Spaghetti with Chicken Parmesan Meatballs 59
  Thigh
    In Green Chili Chicken Enchilada Casserole 127
    In Spicy Chicken Lo Mein 23
    In Sweet and Sour Chicken 25
    In Thai Green Curry 31
Chicken & Dumplings 161
Chicken Parm Sandwich 41
Chicken Quesadillas 123
Chickpeas
  In Falafel Pitas 143
  In Minestrone Soup 169
Chili
  Green
    In Green Chili Chicken Enchilada Casserole 127
  Powder
    In Black Beans Soup 159
    In Chicken Quesadillas 123
    In Classic Beef Tacos 121
    In Fiesta Chicken Burger 43
    In Meaty Mozzarella Pasta Bake 67
    In Skirt Steak Tacos 129
    In Spaghetti with Chicken Parmesan Meatballs 59
    In Steak Fajitas 125
    In Tex-Mex Skillet 133
Chinese Egg Noodles
  In Spicy Chicken Lo Mein 23
Chopped Kale Salad 87
Chuck
  In Pimento Cheeseburgers 53

Ciabatta Buns
  In Chicken Parm Sandwich 41
Cilantro
  In Black Bean Quinoa Burger 37
  In Sticky Pork Sliders 21
  In Thai Green Curry 31
  In Thai Shrimp Salad 97
  In Vegetarian Taco Salad 153
Cinnamon
  In Mediterranean Meatballs 49
Classic Beef Tacos 121
Classic Cobb Salad with Creamy Garlic Dressing 83
Coconut Milk
  In Thai Green Curry 31
Cod Fillets
  In Fish and Chips 105
Coleslaw
  In Sticky Pork Sliders 21
Cooking Grits
  In Shrimp with Bacon & Cheesy Grits 117
Corn
  In Fiesta Chicken Burger 43
  In Pineapple Fried Rice 27
  In Skirt Steak Tacos 129
  In Tex Mex Stuffed Peppers 135
  Tortillas
    In Green Chili Chicken Enchilada Casserole 127
Coriander
  In Falafel Pitas 143
Cornstarch
  In Quick Pepper Steak 29
  In Sweet and Sour Chicken 25
  In Teriyaki Chicken 19
Creole Shrimp Pasta 103
Cucumber
  English

In Banh Mi with Sriracha Mayo 15
   In Greek Salad 85
  In Lemon Chicken Pita Wraps with Tzatziki 45
  In Mediterranean Meatballs 49
  In Raspberry Quinoa Salad 91
  In Tomato, Avocado, and Cucumber Salad 151
  Pickling
    In Sticky Pork Sliders 21
Cumin
  In Black Bean Quinoa Burger 37
  In Black Beans Soup 159
  In Classic Beef Tacos 121
  In Falafel Pitas 143
  In Mediterranean Meatballs 49
  In Steak Fajitas 125
  In Stuffed Poblano Peppers 131
  In Tex-Mex Skillet 133
  In Thai Green Curry 31

D

Dijon Mustard
  In Classic Cobb Salad with Creamy Garlic Dressing 83
  In Dijon Salmon 111
  In Maurice Salad 89
  In Raspberry Quinoa Salad 91
  In Stroganoff Meatballs 71
  In Tex Mex Stuffed Peppers 135
Dijon Salmon 111
Dill
  In Lemon Chicken Pita Wraps with Tzatziki 45
  In Mediterranean Meatballs 49
  In Stroganoff Meatballs 71

E

Egg Drop Soup 163
Edamame
  In Thai Shrimp Salad 97

Egg Noodles
  In Stroganoff Meatballs 71
Eggs
  In Asparagus and Ricotta Frittata 139
  In Black Bean Quinoa Burger 37
  In Broccoli Mushroom Quiche 141
  In Carbonara 57
  In Chicken Parm Sandwich 41
  In Classic Cobb Salad with Creamy Garlic Dressing 83
  In Egg Drop Soup 163
  In Fish and Chips 105
  In Maurice Salad 89
  In Meatball Marinara Submarine Sandwiches 47
  In Mediterranean Meatballs 49
  In Shredded Chicken Caesar Salad 81
  In Spaghetti and Meatballs 69
  In Spaghetti with Chicken Parmesan Meatballs 59
  In Spinach & Ricotta Stuffed Shells 73
Elbow Macaroni
  In Mac and Cheese 63
Escarole
  In Spring Pizza 149

F

Falafel Pitas 143
Fiesta Chicken Burger 43
Fish and Chips 105
Flour
  In Chicken & Dumplings 161
  In Chicken Parm Sandwich 41
  In Creole Shrimp Pasta 103
  In Falafel Pitas 143
  In Fish and Chips 105
  In Gnocchi with Palomino Sauce 145
  In Lightened Cheese Soup 165

Quick and Easy Meals

INDEX

    In Loaded Potato Soup 167
    In Mac and Cheese 63
  Tortillas
        In Chicken Quesadillas 123
        In Skirt Steak Tacos 129
        In Steak Fajitas 125
        In Tex-Mex Skillet 133
  French
    Baguettes
        In Banh Mi with Sriracha Mayo 15
        In Beef Barley Soup 157
  Bread
        In Sausage and Bean Soup 171
  Rolls
        In Meatball Marinara Submarine Sandwiches 47

G

Garlic
  In Aloha BBQ Burger Sliders 35
  In Banh Mi with Sriracha Mayo 15
  In Beef and Broccoli 17
  In Black Bean Quinoa Burger 37
  In Black Beans Soup 159
  In Cajun Shrimp Po' Boy 39
  In Chicken & Dumplings 161
  In Chicken Quesadillas 123
  In Classic Beef Tacos 121
  In Classic Cobb Salad with Creamy Garlic Dressing 83
  In Falafel Pitas 143
  In Fiesta Chicken Burger 43
  In Garlic and Parmesan Salmon 107
  In Gnocchi with Palomino Sauce 145
  In Lemon and Herb Butter Salmon 109
  In Lemon Chicken Pita Wraps with Tzatziki 45
  In Lightened Cheese Soup 165
  In Loaded Potato Soup 167
  In Meatball Marinara Submarine Sandwiches 47
  In Meaty Mozzarella Pasta Bake 67
  In Mediterranean Meatballs 49
  In Minestrone Soup 169
  In Penne with Lemon Cream Sauce and Spinach 61
  In Pimento Cheeseburgers 53
  In Quick Pepper Steak 29
  In Sausage and Bean Soup 171
  In Sausage, Sweet Potato, and Kale Pasta 75
  In Shredded Chicken Caesar Salad 81
  In Shrimp Scampi with Angel Hair 115
  In Skirt Steak Tacos 129
  In Spaghetti and Meatballs 69
  In Spaghetti with Chicken Parmesan Meatballs 59
  In Spicy Chicken Lo Mein 23
  In Spinach & Ricotta Stuffed Shells 73
  In Steak Fajitas 125
  In Sticky Pork Sliders 21
  In Stuffed Cabbage Soup 173
  In Teriyaki Chicken 19
  In Tex-Mex Skillet 133
  In Thai Green Curry 31
  Powder
        In Banh Mi with Sriracha Mayo 15
        In Creole Shrimp Pasta 103
        In Green Chili Chicken Enchilada Casserole 127
        In Orecchiette with Tomato Cream Sauce 65
        In Philly Cheesesteak 51
        In Tex Mex Stuffed Peppers 135
Garlic and Parmesan Salmon 107
Gherkins Pickles
  In Maurice Salad 89
Ginger
  In Thai Green Curry 31

   Powder
      In Banh Mi with Sriracha Mayo 15
      In Beef and Broccoli 17
      In Egg Drop Soup 163
      In Quick Pepper Steak 29
      In Spicy Chicken Lo Mein 23
      In Sticky Pork Sliders 21
      In Sweet and Sour Chicken 25
      In Teriyaki Chicken 19

Gnocchi
  In Gnocchi with Palomino Sauce 145
  In Tomato, Basil, & Gnocchi Soup 175

Gnocchi with Palomino Sauce 145

Greek Salad 85

Greek Yogurt
  In Lemon Chicken Pita Wraps with Tzatziki 45

Green Chili Chicken Enchilada Casserole 127

Green Enchilada Sauce
  In Green Chili Chicken Enchilada Casserole 127

Green Olives
  In Maurice Salad 89

Guacamole
  In Chicken Quesadillas 123
  In Steak Fajitas 125

H

Half & Half
  In Creole Shimp Pasta 103
  In Minestrone Soup 169
  In Sausage and Bean Soup 171

Ham
  In Maurice Salad 89

Hamburger Buns
  In Black Bean Quinoa Burger 37
  In Pimento Cheeseburgers 53

Heavy Cream
  In Carbonara 57
  In Gnocchi with Palomino Sauce 145
  In Penne with Lemon Cream Sauce and Spinach 61
  In Tortellini Alfredo with Bacon 77

Hemp Seeds
  In Chopped Kale Salad 87

Hoagie Rolls
  In Cajun Shrimp Po' Boy 39
  In Philly Cheesesteak 51

Hoisin Sauce
  In Banh Mi with Sriracha Mayo 15

Honey
  In Asian Seared Salmon with Baby Bok Choy 13
  In Raspberry Quinoa Salad 91
  In Sticky Pork Sliders 21
  In Teriyaki Chicken 19

I

Iceberg
  In Vegetarian Taco Salad 153

Italian
  Bread
      In Tomato, Basil, & Gnocchi Soup 175
  Dressing
      In Steak Fajita Salad 95
  Sausage
      In Meaty Mozzarella Pasta Bake 67
      In Orecchiette with Tomato Cream Sauce 65
      In Sausage and Bean Soup 171
      In Sausage, Sweet Potato, and Kale Pasta 75
  Seasoning
      In Orecchiette with Tomato Cream Sauce 65
      In Spaghetti with Chicken Parmesan Meatballs 59

INDEX

J

Jalapeño Chile
  In Banh Mi with Sriracha Mayo 15
  In Sticky Pork Sliders 21
  In Thai Green Curry 31

Jicama
  In Skirt Steak Tacos 129

Jumbo Shells
  In Spinach & Ricotta Stuffed Shells 73

K

Kalamata Olive
  In Greek Salad 85

Kale
  In Chopped Kale Salad 87
  In Raspberry Quinoa Salad 91
  In Sausage and Bean Soup 171
  In Sausage, Sweet Potato, and Kale Pasta 75

Kernel Yellow Corn
  In Steak Fajita Salad 95

Ketchup
  In Sweet and Sour Chicken 25

Kidney Beans
  In Steak Fajita Salad 95
  White of
    In Minestrone Soup 169

L

Leek
  In Asparagus and Ricotta Frittata 139
  In Spring Pizza 149

Lemon Chicken Pita Wraps with Tzatziki 45

Lemon Grass
  In Thai Green Curry 31

Lemon
  In Lemon and Herb Butter Salmon 109
  In Roasted Tandoori Cauliflower 147

  Juice
    In Cajun Shrimp Po' Boy 39
    In Chicken Quesadillas 123
    In Chopped Kale Salad 87
    In Classic Cobb Salad with Creamy Garlic Dressing 83
    In Dijon Salmon 111
    In Lemon and Herb Butter Salmon 109
    In Lemon Chicken Pita Wraps with Tzatziki 45
    In Poached Salmon & Pecan Salad 93
    In Shredded Chicken Caesar Salad 81
    In Steak Fajitas 125

  Zest Of
    In Lemon Chicken Pita Wraps with Tzatziki 45
    In Penne with Lemon Cream Sauce and Spinach 61
    In Steak Fajitas 125

Lemon and Herb Butter Salmon 109

Lettuce
  Iceberg
    In Maurice Salad 89
  In Steak Fajitas 125
  In Stuffed Poblano Peppers 131
  Romaine
    In Cajun Shrimp Po' Boy 39
    In Classic Cobb Salad with Creamy Garlic Dressing 83
    In Thai Shrimp Salad 97

Lightened Cheese Soup 165

Lime
  In Thai Green Curry 31
  Juice
    In Black Bean Quinoa Burger 37
    In Fiesta Chicken Burger 43
    In Skirt Steak Tacos 129
    In Vegetarian Taco Salad 153

Loaded Potato Soup 167

M

Mac and Cheese 63

Marinara Sauce
- In Chicken Parm Sandwich 41
- In Gnocchi with Palomino Sauce 145
- In Meaty Mozzarella Pasta Bake 67
- In Spaghetti with Chicken Parmesan Meatballs 59
- In Spinach & Ricotta Stuffed Shells 73

Maurice Salad 89

Mayo
- In Banh Mi with Sriracha Mayo 15
- In Pimento Cheeseburgers 53

Mayonnaise
- In Cajun Shrimp Po' Boy 39
- In Classic Cobb Salad with Creamy Garlic Dressing 83
- In Fiesta Chicken Burger 43
- In Maurice Salad 89
- In Shredded Chicken Caesar Salad 81

Meatball Marinara Submarine Sandwiches 47

Meaty Mozzarella Pasta Bake 67

Mediterranean Meatballs 49

Mexican Stewed Tomatoes
- In Tex-Mex Skillet 133
- In Vegetarian Taco Salad 153

Milk
- In Asparagus and Ricotta Frittata 139
- In Gnocchi with Palomino Sauce 145
- In Loaded Potato Soup 167
- In Mac and Cheese 63
- In Stroganoff Meatballs 71

Minestrone Soup 169

Mozzarella
- In Meaty Mozzarella Pasta Bake 67
- In Spaghetti with Chicken Parmesan Meatballs 59

Mushroom

Baby Bella
- In Beef Barley Soup 157
- In Broccoli Mushroom Quiche 141
- In Stroganoff Meatballs 71

N

Napa Cabbage
- In Thai Shrimp Salad 97

Navy Beans
- In Sausage and Bean Soup 171

Nutritional Yeast
- In Black Bean Quinoa Burger 37
- In Chopped Kale Salad 87

O

Oil
- In Raspberry Quinoa Salad 91
- In Shredded Chicken Caesar Salad 81

Old Bay®
- In Fish and Chips 105
- In Shrimp with Bacon & Cheesy Grits 117

Olive Oil
- In Cajun Shrimp Po' Boy 39
- In Chopped Kale Salad 87
- In Lemon Chicken Pita Wraps with Tzatziki 45
- In Meatball Marinara Submarine Sandwiches 47

Onion

Green
- In Banh Mi with Sriracha Mayo 15
- In Egg Drop Soup 163
- In Greek Salad 85
- In Loaded Potato Soup 167
- In Pineapple Fried Rice 27
- In Shrimp with Bacon & Cheesy Grits 117
- In Skirt Steak Tacos 129
- In Sticky Pork Sliders 21

INDEX

    In Sweet and Sour Chicken 25
    In Teriyaki Chicken 19
    In Thai Green Curry 31
    In Thai Shrimp Salad 97
    In Tomato, Avocado, and Cucumber Salad 151
    In Tomato Beet Salad 99
In Beef Barley Soup 157
In Beef and Broccoli 17
In Black Beans Soup 159
In Broccoli Mushroom Quiche 141
In Chicken & Dumplings 161
In Chicken Quesadillas 123
In Classic Beef Tacos 121
In Gnocchi with Palomino Sauce 145
In Lightened Cheese Soup 165
In Loaded Potato Soup 167
In Minestrone Soup 169
In Pineapple Fried Rice 27
In Quick Pepper Steak 29
In Spicy Chicken Lo Mein 23
In Steak Fajitas 125
In Stroganoff Meatballs 71
In Stuffed Cabbage Soup 173
In Stuffed Poblano Peppers 131
In Tex-Mex Skillet 133
In Tex Mex Stuffed Peppers 135
Powder
    In Aloha BBQ Burger Sliders 35
    In Beef Barley Soup 157
    In Chicken Quesadillas 123
    In Creole Shrimp Pasta 103
    In Green Chili Chicken Enchilada Casserole 127
    In Sausage and Bean Soup 171
    In Skirt Steak Tacos 129
    In Pimento Cheeseburgers 53
Red

  In Aloha BBQ Burger Sliders 35
  In Black Bean Quinoa Burger 37
  In Cajun Shrimp Po' Boy 39
  In Chopped Kale Salad 87
  In Falafel Pitas 143
  In Philly Cheesesteak 51
  In Sausage, Sweet Potato, and Kale Pasta 75
  In Steak Fajita Salad 95
Orecchiette Pasta
  In Orecchiette with Tomato Cream Sauce 65
  In Sausage, Sweet Potato, and Kale Pasta 75
Orecchiette with Tomato Cream Sauce 65
Oregano
  In Black Beans Soup 159
  In Cajun Shrimp Po' Boy 39
  In Creole Shrimp Pasta 103
  In Lemon Chicken Pita Wraps with Tzatziki 45
  In Meatball Marinara Submarine Sandwiches 47
  In Mediterranean Meatballs 49
  In Raspberry Quinoa Salad 91
  In Spaghetti and Meatballs 69
  In Spaghetti with Chicken Parmesan Meatballs 59
  In Tex Mex Stuffed Peppers 135
  In Tomato, Basil, & Gnocchi Soup 175
Oyster Sauce
  In Beef and Broccoli 17
  In Spicy Chicken Lo Mein 23

P

Pearl Barley
  In Beef Barley Soup 157
Panko Breadcrumbs
  In Black Bean Quinoa Burger 37
  In Chicken Parm Sandwich 41
  In Fish and Chips 105

In Mac and Cheese 63
In Tortellini Alfredo with Bacon 77
Paprika
  In Aloha BBQ Burger Sliders 35
  In Cajun Shrimp Po' Boy 39
  In Creole Shrimp Pasta 103
  In Fish and Chips 105
  In Mac and Cheese 63
  In Steak Fajitas 125
  In Stuffed Cabbage Soup 173
  In Tex Mex Stuffed Peppers 135
Parmesan
  In Carbonara 57
  In Penne with Lemon Cream Sauce and Spinach 61
  In Sausage, Sweet Potato, and Kale Pasta 75
  In Spinach & Ricotta Stuffed Shells 73
  In Tomato, Avocado, and Cucumber Salad 151
  In Tortellini Alfredo with Bacon 77
Parsley
  In Beef Barley Soup 157
  In Creole Shrimp Pasta 103
  In Dijon Salmon 111
  In Falafel Pitas 143
  In Garlic and Parmesan Salmon 107
  In Lemon and Herb Butter Salmon 109
  In Mediterranean Meatballs 49
  In Minestrone Soup 169
  In Orecchiette with Tomato Cream Sauce 65
  In Shrimp Scampi with Angel Hair 115
Pasta 54
  In Minestrone Soup 169
Peas
  In Pineapple Fried Rice 27
Pecans
  In Poached Salmon & Pecan Salad 93
  In Raspberry Quinoa Salad 91
Penne Pasta
  In Creole Shrimp Pasta 103
  In Penne with Lemon Cream Sauce and Spinach 61
Penne with Lemon Cream Sauce and Spinach 61
Pepper
  Black
    In Cajun Shrimp Po' Boy 39
    In Classic Cobb Salad with Creamy Garlic Dressing 83
    In Creole Shrimp Pasta 103
    In Philly Cheesesteak 51
  Cayenne
    In Black Beans Soup 159
    In Cajun Shrimp Po' Boy 39
    In Chopped Kale Salad 87
    In Classic Beef Tacos 121
    In Creole Shrimp Pasta 103
    In Fiesta Chicken Burger 43
    In Pimento Cheeseburgers 53
  Chili
    In Black Bean Quinoa Burger 37
    In Tex Mex Stuffed Peppers 135
  Green
    In Philly Cheesesteak 51
    In Quick Pepper Steak 29
    In Steak Fajitas 125
    In Steak Fajita Salad 95
  In Aloha Bbq Burger Sliders 35
  In Asian Seared Salmon with Baby Bok Choy 13
  In Beef Barley Soup 157
  In Black Bean Quinoa Burger 37
  In Black Beans Soup 159
  In Broccoli Mushroom Quiche 141
  In Carbonara 57
  In Chicken & Dumplings 161
  In Chicken Parm Sandwich 41
  In Chicken Quesadillas 123
  In Egg Drop Soup 163

Quick and Easy Meals **191**

INDEX

In Greek Salad 85
In Lemon Chicken Pita Wraps with Tzatziki 45
In Loaded Potato Soup 167
In Meatball Marinara Submarine Sandwiches 47
In Meaty Mozzarella Pasta Bake 67
In Mediterranean Meatballs 49
In Minestrone Soup 169
In Penne with Lemon Cream Sauce and Spinach 61
In Pimento Cheeseburgers 53
In Raspberry Quinoa Salad 91
In Sausage and Bean Soup 171
In Sausage, Sweet Potato, and Kale Pasta 75
In Shredded Chicken Caesar Salad 81
In Shrimp Scampi with Angel Hair 115
In Skirt Steak Tacos 129
In Stroganoff Meatballs 71
In Stuffed Cabbage Soup 173
In Sweet and Sour Chicken 25
In Teriyaki Chicken 19
In Tex Mex Stuffed Peppers 135
In Thai Green Curry 31
In Tomato, Avocado, and Cucumber Salad 151
Poblano
    In Stuffed Poblano Peppers 131
Red Bell
    In Chicken Quesadillas 123
    In Chopped Kale Salad 87
    In Philly Cheesesteak 51
    In Spicy Chicken Lo Mein 23
    In Steak Fajitas 125
    In Steak Fajita Salad 95
    In Stuffed Cabbage Soup 173
    In Sweet and Sour Chicken 25
Philly Cheesesteak 51
Pickled Beets
In Greek Salad 85
In Tomato Beet Salad 99
Pie Crust
  In Broccoli Mushroom Quiche 141
Pimentos
  In Pimento Cheeseburgers 53
Pimento Cheeseburgers 53
Pineapple Fried Rice 27
Pineapple
  In Aloha BBQ Burger Sliders 35
  In Pineapple Fried Rice 27
  Juice
    In Sweet and Sour Chicken 25
Pinto Beans
  In Vegetarian Taco Salad 153
Pita Flatbreads
  In Lemon Chicken Pita Wraps with Tzatziki 45
  In Mediterranean Meatballs 49
Pita Pockets
  In Falafel Pitas 143
Pizza Dough
  In Spring Pizza 149
Poached Salmon & Pecan Salad 93
Pork
  Shoulder Roast
    In Sticky Pork Sliders 21
  Tenderloin
    In Banh Mi with Sriracha Mayo 15
Potato
  Russet
    In Fish and Chips 105
    In Loaded Potato Soup 167
  Sweet
    In Sausage, Sweet Potato, and Kale Pasta 75
Poultry Seasoning
  In Beef Barley Soup 157
  In Chicken & Dumplings 161

Q

Quinoa
　In Black Bean Quinoa Burger 37
　In Chopped Kale Salad 87
　In Raspberry Quinoa Salad 91
Quick Pepper Steak 29

R

Radishes
　In Poached Salmon & Pecan Salad 93
Raspberry
　In Raspberry Quinoa Salad 91
Raspberry Quinoa Salad 91
Red Wine Vinegar
　In Tomato, Avocado, and Cucumber Salad 151
　In Raspberry Quinoa Salad 91
Rice
　In Black Beans Soup 159
　In Stuffed Poblano Peppers 131
　In Tex-Mex Skillet 133
Rice Vinegar
　In Banh Mi with Sriracha Mayo 15
　In Egg Drop Soup 163
Rice Wine Vinegar
　In Beef and Broccoli 17
　In Classic Cobb Salad with Creamy Garlic Dressing 83
　In Sticky Pork Sliders 21
　In Sweet and Sour Chicken 25
　In Teriyaki Chicken 19
Ricotta
　In Spinach & Ricotta Stuffed Shells 73
Roasted Tandoori Cauliflower 147
Romaine Hearts
　In Raspberry Quinoa Salad 91
　In Shredded Chicken Caesar Salad 81
　In Vegetarian Taco Salad 153
Rosemary
　In Mediterranean Meatballs 49

S

Salad Green
　In Steak Fajita Salad 95
Salad Oil
　In Classic Cobb Salad with Creamy Garlic Dressing 83
Salads 78
Salmon Fillets
　In Asian Seared Salmon with Baby Bok Choy 13
　In Dijon Salmon 111
　In Garlic and Parmesan Salmon 107
　In Lemon and Herb Butter Salmon 109
　In Poached Salmon & Pecan Salad 93
Salsa
　In Chicken Quesadillas 123
　In Stuffed Poblano Peppers 131
Salt
　In Aloha BBQ Burger Sliders 35
　In Beef Barley Soup 157
　In Black Bean Quinoa Burger 37
　In Black Beans Soup 159
　In Broccoli Mushroom Quiche 141
　In Cajun Shrimp Po' Boy 39
　In Carbonara 57
　In Chicken & Dumplings 161
　In Chicken Parm Sandwich 41
　In Chicken Quesadillas 123
　In Dijon Salmon 111
　In Egg Drop Soup 163
　In Fiesta Chicken Burger 43
　In Gnocchi with Palomino Sauce 145
　In Green Chili Chicken Enchilada Casserole 127
　In Lemon Chicken Pita Wraps with Tzatziki 45
　In Loaded Potato Soup 167
　In Maurice Salad 89
　In Meaty Mozzarella Pasta Bake 67

INDEX

In Mediterranean Meatballs 49
In Minestrone Soup 169
In Penne with Lemon Cream Sauce and Spinach 61
In Philly Cheesesteak 51
In Raspberry Quinoa Salad 91
In Sausage and Bean Soup 171
In Skirt Steak Tacos 129
In Spaghetti with Chicken Parmesan Meatballs 59
In Stroganoff Meatballs 71
In Stuffed Cabbage Soup 173
In Sweet and Sour Chicken 25
In Teriyaki Chicken 19
In Tex Mex Stuffed Peppers 135
In Thai Green Curry 31
In Tomato, Avocado, and Cucumber Salad 151
In Tomato, Basil, & Gnocchi Soup 175
Sausage and Bean Soup 171
Sausage, Sweet Potato, and Kale Pasta 75
Scallions
  In Poached Salmon & Pecan Salad 93
Seafood 100
Seasoned Whitefish with Sun-Dried Tomatoes & Spinach 113
Sesame
  Oil
    In Asian Seared Salmon with Baby Bok Choy 13
    In Banh Mi with Sriracha Mayo 15
    In Beef and Broccoli 17
    In Egg Drop Soup 163
    In Spicy Chicken Lo Mein 23
    In Teriyaki Chicken 19
  Seeds
    In Asian Seared Salmon with Baby Bok Choy 13
    In Teriyaki Chicken 19
    In Thai Shrimp Salad 97

Sherry
  In Sticky Pork Sliders 21
  In Teriyaki Chicken 19
Shredded Chicken Caesar Salad 81
Shrimp
  In Cajun Shrimp Po' Boy 39
  In Creole Shrimp Pasta 103
  In Shrimp with Bacon & Cheesy Grits 117
  In Thai Shrimp Salad 97
Shrimp Scampi with Angel Hair 115
Shrimp with Bacon & Cheesy Grits 117
Sirloin
  In Beef and Broccoli 17
  In Philly Cheesesteak 51
  Steak
    In Steak Fajitas 125
    In Quick Pepper Steak 29
  In Steak Fajita Salad 95
Skirt Steak
  In Skirt Steak Tacos 129
Skirt Steak Tacos 129
Snow Peas
  In Egg Drop Soup 163
  In Sweet and Sour Chicken 25
  In Teriyaki Chicken 19
  In Thai Green Curry 31
Soups 155
Sour Cream
  In Chicken Quesadillas 123
  In Green Chili Chicken Enchilada Casserole 127
  In Loaded Potato Soup 167
  In Steak Fajitas 125
  In Stroganoff Meatballs 71
  In Stuffed Poblano Peppers 131
  In Vegetarian Taco Salad 153
Soy Sauce
  In Asian Seared Salmon with Baby Bok Choy 13

In Banh Mi with Sriracha Mayo 15
In Beef and Broccoli 17
In Egg Drop Soup 163
In Philly Cheesesteak 51
In Quick Pepper Steak 29
In Spicy Chicken Lo Mein 23
In Sticky Pork Sliders 21
In Teriyaki Chicken 19
In Thai Green Curry 31

Spaghetti
  In Carbonara 57

Spaghetti and Meatballs 69

Spaghetti Noodles
  In Spaghetti and Meatballs 69
  In Spaghetti with Chicken Parmesan Meatballs 59

Spaghetti with Chicken Parmesan Meatballs 59

Spicy Chicken Lo Mein 23

Spinach
  Baby Of
    In Classic Cobb Salad with Creamy Garlic Dressing 83
    In Minestrone Soup 169
    In Spinach & Ricotta Stuffed Shells 73
    In Penne with Lemon Cream Sauce and Spinach 61
  In Seasoned Whitefish with Sun-Dried Tomatoes & Spinach 113

Spinach & Ricotta Stuffed Shells 73

Spring Mix
  In Poached Salmon & Pecan Salad 93

Spring Pizza 149

Sriracha
  In Banh Mi with Sriracha Mayo 15

Sriracha Chili Sauce
  In Spicy Chicken Lo Mein 23

Steak Fajitas 125

Steak Fajita Salad 95

Stew Meat
  In Beef Barley Soup 157

Sticky Pork Sliders 21

Stroganoff Meatballs 71

Stuffed Cabbage Soup 173

Stuffed Poblano Peppers 131

Sugar
  Brown
    In Banh Mi with Sriracha Mayo 15
    In Beef and Broccoli 17
    In Poached Salmon & Pecan Salad 93
    In Steak Fajitas 125
    In Sticky Pork Sliders 21
    In Sweet and Sour Chicken 25
    In Thai Green Curry 31
  In Banh Mi with Sriracha Mayo 15
  In Classic Cobb Salad with Creamy Garlic Dressing 83
  In Maurice Salad 89
  In Quick Pepper Steak 29
  In Skirt Steak Tacos 129
  In Spicy Chicken Lo Mein 23
  In Sticky Pork Sliders 21

Sweet and Sour Chicken 25

Sweet Corn
  In Chicken Quesadillas 123

Sweet Dinner Rolls
  In Aloha BBQ Burger Sliders 35

Sweet Pickle Relish
  In Cajun Shrimp Po' Boy 39

Swiss Cheese
  In Aloha Bbq Burger Sliders 35

T

Taco Sauce
  In Stuffed Poblano Peppers 131

Tandoori Paste
  In Roasted Tandoori Cauliflower 147

INDEX

Teriyaki Chicken 19
Tex Mex 118
Tex-Mex Skillet 133
Tex Mex Stuffed Peppers 135
Thai Green Curry 31
Thai Shrimp Salad 97
Thyme
  In Aloha BBQ Burger Sliders 35
  In Beef Barley Soup 157
  In Cajun Shrimp Po' Boy 39
  In Creole Shrimp Pasta 103
Tomato
  Cherry
    In Spring Pizza 149
    In Steak Fajita Salad 95
    In Tomato, Avocado, and Cucumber Salad 151
  Grape
    In Skirt Steak Tacos 129
  In Black Beans Soup 159
  In Cajun Shrimp Po' Boy 39
  In Chopped Kale Salad 87
  In Classic Cobb Salad with Creamy Garlic Dressing 83
  In Greek Salad 85
  In Lemon Chicken Pita Wraps with Tzatziki 45
  In Meatball Marinara Submarine Sandwiches 47
  In Mediterranean Meatballs 49
  In Minestrone Soup 169
  In Orecchiette with Tomato Cream Sauce 65
  In Seasoned Whitefish with Sun-Dried Tomatoes & Spinach 113
  In Spaghetti and Meatballs 69
  In Tomato, Basil, & Gnocchi Soup 175
  Juice
    In Stuffed Cabbage Soup 173
  Heirloom
    In Tomato Beet Salad 99
  Paste
    In Classic Beef Tacos 121
    In Minestrone Soup 169
  Puree
    In Meatball Marinara Submarine Sandwiches 47
    In Spaghetti and Meatballs 69
  Sauce
    In Orecchiette with Tomato Cream Sauce 65
Tomato Beet Salad 99
Tomato, Avocado, And Cucumber Salad 151
Tomato, Basil, & Gnocchi Soup 175
Tortellini Alfredo with Bacon 77
Tortillas
  In Classic Beef Tacos 121
  In Vegetarian Taco Salad 153
Tri-Colored Tortilla
  In Steak Fajita Salad 95
Turkey Breast
  In Maurice Salad 89

V

Vanilla Extract
  In Poached Salmon & Pecan Salad 93
Vegetarian 136
Vegetarian Taco Salad 153
Vinegar
  In Maurice Salad 89z

W

Water
  In Asian Seared Salmon with Baby Bok Choy 13
  In Beef Barley Soup 157
  In Beef and Broccoli 17
  In Chicken & Dumplings 161
  In Egg Drop Soup 163
  In Lightened Cheese Soup 165

In Meatball Marinara Submarine Sandwiches 47

  In Quick Pepper Steak 29

  In Roasted Tandoori Cauliflower 147

  In Sausage and Bean Soup 171

  In Spaghetti and Meatballs 69

  In Stuffed Cabbage Soup 173

  In Stuffed Poblano Peppers 131

  In Sweet and Sour Chicken 25

  In Teriyaki Chicken 19

  In Thai Green Curry 31

Water Chestnuts

  In Spicy Chicken Lo Mein 23

  In Thai Shrimp Salad 97

White Wine

  In Shrimp Scampi with Angel Hair 115

Wonton Strips

  In Thai Shrimp Salad 97

Worcestershire Sauce

  In Black Bean Quinoa Burger 37

  In Cajun Shrimp Po' Boy 39

  In Classic Cobb Salad with Creamy Garlic Dressing 83

  In Philly Cheesesteak 51

  In Shredded Chicken Caesar Salad 81

  In Stroganoff Meatballs 71

  In Stuffed Cabbage Soup 173

Y-Z

Yellow Squash

  In Minestrone Soup 169

Zucchini

  In Minestrone Soup 169